HOME DESIGN WORKBOOKS
KITCHEN

HOME DESIGN WORKBOOKS
KITCHEN

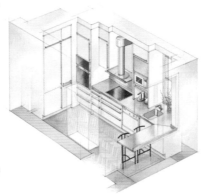

JOHNNY GREY

I(T)P® **Nelson**

an International Thomson Publishing company

Toronto • Albany • Bonn • Boston • Cincinnati • Detroit • London • Madrid • Melbourne
Mexico City • New York • Pacific Grove • Paris • San Francisco • Singapore • Tokyo • Washington

I(T)P® International Thomson Publishing
The ITP logo is a trademark under licence

For Harry, Felix, Augusta and Benedict – who may find it useful someday.

Project Editor BELLA PRINGLE
Project Art Editor COLIN WALTON
Picture Research JULIA PASHLEY
Location Photography PETER ANDERSON
Studio Photography MATTHEW WARD
Stylists MICHELLE AND YVONNE ROBERTS
Production Controller ALISON JONES
Senior Managing Editor MARY-CLARE JERRAM
Managing Art Editor AMANDA LUNN

Published in 1997 by
I(T)P Nelson
A division of Thomson Canada Limited
1120 Birchmount Road, Scarborough, Ontario M1K 5G4

First published in Great Britain in 1997 by Dorling Kindersley Limited
9 Henrietta Street, London WC2E 8PS

Copyright © 1997 Dorling Kindersley Limited, London
Text copyright © 1997 Johnny Grey

Canadian Cataloguing in Publication Data

Grey, Johnny
    Kitchen

(ITP Nelson home design workbooks)
ISBN 0-17-606824-4

1. Kitchens.   2. Interior decoration.   I. Title.
II. Series

NK2117.K5G73 1996   747.7'97   C96-932427-8

Text film output in Great Britain by Optigraph
Reproduced in Singapore by Pica
Printed in Great Britain by Butler and Tanner

Room Plans · 48

Plan Your Design · 74

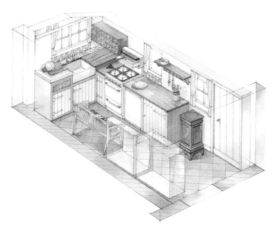

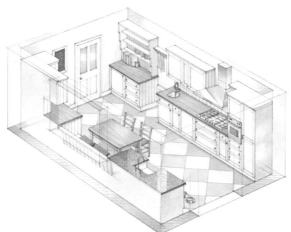

CONTENTS

INTRODUCTION

△ **DISTINCTIVE SURFACES**
Hand-crafted details, such
as this wood door with its
"suitcase" handle and inlaid
surround, contribute to the
atmosphere of a kitchen.

FOR MANY OF US, the kitchen is the most
used room in the house. It is not just a
refueling station, but the place where
adults congregate and children naturally migrate,
and not just for food but company.

I recall with great affection the small, chaotic
family kitchen in our London house where my
mother cooked for the seven of us, and where we
ate most meals. Although the kitchen was very
cramped, low-ceilinged, and dark, and contained
a gigantic, noisy refrigerator that took up about a
quarter of the space, mealtimes were memorable

for their animated conversations and laughter.
To my mind, too few kitchens seem to be able
to combine successful planning with the warm
atmosphere I remember from my childhood.

Reconciling practical considerations – such as
where appliances and furniture should be placed
so that they are efficient to use – with comfort is
hard, but this reconciliation is the mainstay of
ergonomic design. In *Kitchen*, I have tried to
show you how to achieve a balance that works
for you, whether you are designing a brand-new
kitchen or simply remodeling an existing one.

CREATIVE SPACE ▷
The lived-in appearance of
Elizabeth David's kitchen
was a source of inspiration
to me. Through her, I
discovered that kitchens
could be comfortably
furnished, like any other
room in the house.

◁ DISH STORAGE
Keep an open mind when
choosing kitchen elements.
A cupboard for storing
crockery may be more in
keeping with your design
than fitted kitchen cabinets.

into purchasing appliances, cabinets, and other
fittings that look attractive in catalogs but do not
suit your lifestyle or cooking habits. "A good
meal is never expensive but a bad one always is."
So the saying goes, and it is these costly mistakes
that I intend to help you avoid.

The three major expenses when installing a
kitchen are furniture, appliances, and labor. It
is important to assess your budget and decide
which expenses should be given priority. In my
opinion, it is better to have fewer pieces of
furniture made to a high standard, with perhaps
a make-do cupboard that can be removed at a
later date, than a complete kitchen made from
cheap, low-quality cabinets that will not last.

△ STAINLESS STEEL
Think carefully before
selecting a kitchen cabinet
finish. An industrial material
such as this is heat- and
water-resistant, and reflects
light, brightening the room.

Having been involved in kitchen design for the
past 18 years, and having come into contact with
the needs of many individuals and families, I
have developed a great deal of affection for the
kitchen as well as knowledge about its design.
Early on, much of this enthusiasm came through
the influence of my late aunt, the cooking writer
Elizabeth David. She was the person who first
pointed out to me that kitchens do not need to
be plastic laminate boxes, carefully arranged
around the perimeter walls. Her kitchen was
highly atmospheric, almost a study (she wrote
many of her books at its scrubbed pine table)
but also a living room, and all this at a time
during the 1950s and 1960s when its design
was completely out of step with the fashion.
Today, we have come full circle. Our idea of
the kitchen as a place to live in, relax, and be
sociable, as well as cook, would have pleased her.

Designing a kitchen is usually the biggest
financial investment after buying a house or an
apartment, and it is all too easy to be seduced

KITCHEN ACTIVITIES

Start by deciding what you will be doing and
how much time you want to spend in your new
kitchen. Do you want to use it just for cooking
the occasional meal, for professional cooking, or
would you like it to be the main family room in
the house? I've found that many of my clients
prefer kitchens that contain not only a cooking
area but an informal dining area, where adults
can entertain and children can do their
homework, draw, or paint. They also request a

"soft" area with a
carpet for children
to play on, a sofa
and television, and
a kitchen desk for
dealing with home
administration and
telephone calls.

COOL STORAGE ▷
Consider a larder for storing
fresh produce rather than
relying just on a refrigerator.

◁ UTENSIL RACK
A wrought-iron rack above a stove or food preparation area offers easy access to kitchen utensils. It also makes an attractive display.

In order to produce a successful kitchen design that matches your needs, you have to go back to fundamentals. First establish what you enjoy and what you dislike about your existing kitchen, and use the ideas here to help build a picture of your ideal kitchen. Consider how you move around the room: how far do you have to travel from the refrigerator to the preparation area? Are storage cabinets difficult to reach? Are there work surfaces close to the stove? Is it easy to carry in grocery bags from the car?

Once you have worked out how you are going to use the space, research the features that best suit your needs. In the chapter featuring *Kitchen Elements*, the pros and cons of the major kitchen appliances are outlined. For example, if you cook with plenty of fresh ingredients you will be able to judge whether a pantry or a jumbo-sized

△ GLASS BACKSPLASH
As an alternative to tiles, consider using glass to protect walls near stoves.

WHAT DO YOU WANT FROM YOUR KITCHEN?

Before committing yourself to expensive cabinets and equipment, assess your lifestyle and the kind of noncooking activities you wish to undertake in your new kitchen. Use the following options to help you decide what type of kitchen will suit you best.

❶ A ROOM SOLELY FOR COOKING MEALS WITHOUT INTERRUPTION.

❷ A FAMILY ROOM WHERE LIGHT MEALS ARE EATEN.

❸ A KITCHEN THAT DOUBLES AS A DINING ROOM.

❹ A SPACE FOR PROFESSIONAL CATERING ON A LARGE SCALE.

❺ A ROOM FOR RESEARCHING, WRITING, AND PLANNING MENUS.

❻ AN AREA WHERE CHILDREN CAN PLAY AND DO HOMEWORK.

◁ KITCHEN USES
A desk area for organizing household activities has been designed into this family kitchen. One wall is devoted to a desk with shelves above, a bulletin board, and a blackboard.

HOW SUITABLE IS YOUR ROOM?

Before you decide to spend a lot of money on remodeling an existing kitchen, or on designing one from scratch for a new home, make sure that the room you choose to be the kitchen has the necessary features or can be easily adapted.

☐ Is the total space big enough for you and your family? Could the room be extended?

☐ Does the room have access to other associated rooms such as the pantry, utility room, and dining room? Is it possible to add or move the doors in order to improve the link?

☐ Does the room adjoin the yard so that you can have an outdoor dining area in summer, watch while your children play outside, or keep the kitchen door open for extra ventilation?

☐ Does the room under consideration have easy or direct access to the garage or parking area for unloading shopping?

☐ Is the natural light good? Could lighting be improved by adding a new window?

☐ Are there enough electrical outlets in the right places? Could new plumbing be added?

refrigerator is a better investment. Whatever the dimensions of your kitchen, try to limit the number of elements to keep the plan simple. In small kitchens, durable items that offer several uses may be better than specialized features that have only an occasional use. The same applies to small gadgets and electrical appliances whose limited uses may not justify the amount of space they occupy in the room.

KITCHEN CHARACTER

The personality of a room is determined by the individual elements. In kitchens, these elements also have to be functional because they are used more intensively than other household furniture, and come into daily contact with heat and water. Stainless-steel refrigerators and counters, for example, contribute an air of professionalism to the domestic kitchen because this highly durable

material is frequently used in restaurant kitchens. Wood cabinets, on the other hand, or utensils hanging from racks, can provide the warm atmosphere associated with country kitchens.

It is not only kitchen appliances that matter. Other details, such as your choice of counters, lighting, cabinet finishes, wall coverings, and flooring, all present an opportunity to influence the character of the room and contribute to a comfortable kitchen environment. When choosing these elements, bear in mind both aesthetic and practical considerations. Kitchen flooring, for example, needs to be easy to clean, hard wearing, and soft underfoot, as well as beautiful to look at, while a well-thought-out mix of task lighting and soft ambient lighting can make all the difference to working and eating areas. For kitchen cabinets, the quality of craftsmanship and choice of materials are vital

QUALITY FINISHES ▷
Buy the best-quality
cabinets you can afford.
Good craftsmanship is a
sensible investment as it
ages particularly well.

WHAT COULD YOU CHANGE?

Use the following
checklist to help you
pinpoint what it is
about your kitchen
that you would like
to improve or replace.
☐ Change shape of
existing room.
☐ Alter architectural
features.
☐ Improve access to
natural light.
☐ Reorganize layout of
kitchen cabinets.
☐ Upgrade major
appliances.
☐ Increase number of
electrical outlets.
☐ Redesign lighting.
☐ Relocate plumbing.
☐ Reorganize available
storage space.
☐ Rethink the size and
height of counters.
☐ Change countertop
materials.
☐ Replace flooring.
☐ Renew wall coverings
and backsplashes.
☐ Alter style of cabinets
and door handles.
☐ Rehinge entry doors.
☐ Change furniture.
☐ Update all curtains,
blinds, wall coverings,
and floorings.
☐ Decrease noise levels.

if they are to withstand daily wear and tear. Also,
by choosing from a range of gloss or matte, pale
or dark, cabinet finishes, you can affect how the
cabinets reflect natural light in the kitchen room.

KITCHEN LAYOUT

For me, kitchen planning falls into two distinct
categories, built-in and "unfitted." Built-in
kitchens, developed in the 1950s as the "dream"
solution to kitchen design, rely upon cabinets
placed against the walls, while unfitted types use
freestanding elements to furnish the room.

The "unfitted" approach particularly interests
me, and it is an area of kitchen planning that I
pioneered throughout the 1980s. It has grown in

popularity, as for many individuals the warm,
comfortable appearance of these kitchens is easier
both to live with and to work in. The Family
Kitchen (*below*) is an example of this planning.
By grouping all the cooking and preparation
facilities together, fewer elements have to be
placed around the walls, leaving space for a table,
a sofa, and doors opening out onto the yard.

Above all, the purpose of this book is to
explain how to arrive at an ergonomic kitchen
design where the user feels comfortable. Whether
your kitchen is large or small, it will help you
choose appliances and furniture according to
your needs, and arrange them for ease of use, in a
way that is not only practical but looks wonderful.

CHANGING THE SHAPE ▷
To create a large family room
with space for sitting, dining,
and desk areas, three smaller
rooms have been combined.

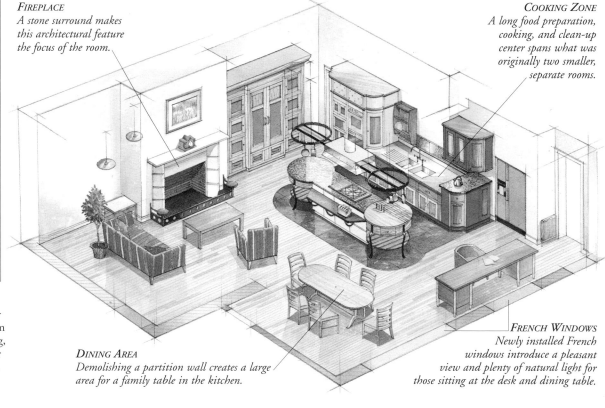

FIREPLACE
A stone surround makes
this architectural feature
the focus of the room.

COOKING ZONE
A long food preparation,
cooking, and clean-up
center spans what was
originally two smaller,
separate rooms.

DINING AREA
Demolishing a partition wall creates a large
area for a family table in the kitchen.

FRENCH WINDOWS
Newly installed French
windows introduce a pleasant
view and plenty of natural light for
those sitting at the desk and dining table.

PLAN OF ACTION

Before you go ahead with your renovations, use this checklist to ensure that you have not overlooked any requirements. A date for completion and good coordination of plumbers, electricians, and other contractors is also important. Consider the following:

☐ Have you obtained construction permits for any structural alterations?

☐ Can you afford the time to do some of the work yourself?

☐ Will you need professional help?

☐ Have you estimated the costs accurately and allowed a little extra?

☐ Have you left enough money for finishing decoration and fixtures?

☐ Is this amount of work within your budget or are you happy to keep some features as they are?

☐ Will your plans increase the resale value of the property?

☐ Have you made other plans for eating when work is in progress?

◁ **KITCHEN CARE**
A finished kitchen needs regular maintenance to keep it looking its best. Here, wood counters have been oiled, wood floors varnished, and cabinet doors repainted.

ASSESS YOUR NEEDS

THE FOLLOWING questions will help you focus on your specific kitchen needs and think about ways to approach kitchen planning so that, as you work through the book, you will be able to compile a list of the kitchen elements and designs that suit you best.

STORAGE

The number of people you cook for, how many meals you cook at home, the type of foods you use, how you shop, and who needs access to storage, determine the type and amount of storage space you need in your kitchen.

■ FOOD:

☐ Do you cook with a mixture of fresh, frozen, chilled, dried, preserved, or canned foods, or does one type predominate?
☐ Do you have enough refrigerator, freezer, and cabinet space to house your preferred choice of cooking ingredients?
☐ If you cook with mainly fresh ingredients, do you have cool, well-ventilated storage for vegetables and fruit, or do you rely solely on the refrigerator?
☐ If you like to prepare meals well in advance and freeze them, do you have enough storage space in your freezer?
☐ Do you not use a car, work all day, live far from the grocery store, so that you need more than the average amount of storage space?
☐ Do you buy essential items in bulk and need additional space to keep large packages, cans, and bottles?
☐ Do you store bottles of good wine and so need an even temperature site away from the stove?
☐ Are your food storage facilities, such as the refrigerator and pantry, within a few steps of food preparation areas to save journeys across the kitchen?
☐ Are items of food well organized so that they are easy to find, not lost or forgotten at the back of kitchen cabinets?
☐ Do you expend unnecessary energy reaching up to pick cooking ingredients off high shelves, or bending down to reach into cabinets below counter level? If so, could you reorganize your storage cabinets more efficiently so that frequently used items are kept somewhere between knee height and eye level?

☐ If you have young children, do you want some high storage areas to keep certain rationed foods, such as candy and cookies, out of reach?

■ EQUIPMENT:

☐ Have you accumulated a huge amount of kitchen equipment that needs storing? If so, have you sorted out the equipment to check that every item is useful?
☐ Are there any less frequently used items, such as an ice-cream maker, that could be kept out of the way on high shelves?
☐ Have you allowed room to store everyday food preparation equipment within reach of food preparation areas?
☐ Is there space for heavy food processors, toasters, and juicers to be kept plugged in at the back of countertops?
☐ Can cooking utensils be stored close to the stovetop?
☐ Can cutting boards and knives be stored within reach of food preparation areas?
☐ Can pans and baking trays be stored near the oven?
☐ Are your day-to-day plates, glasses, and cutlery close to the eating area for setting the table, or close to the dishwasher?
☐ Have you allowed space to store non-food associated items such as cleaning and shoe-polishing products, in the kitchen?

FOOD PREPARATION

An efficient work space for food preparation demands careful planning. Think about its location in relation to other activity areas, the type of food you prepare, the number of people you cook for on a daily basis, and whether you need extra preparation areas for others to share the work.

☐ How much day-to-day wear are your food preparation counters subjected to? Do you prepare several meals at home daily, or do you often eat out? Do you cook for just yourself, for yourself and your partner, or do you have a family to feed?
☐ Do you prepare food on your own, or do your partner and children share the work and space with you? If children are involved in food preparation, would a low-level work area be useful?
☐ Do you cook mainly with fresh food that requires lots of preparation space, or a high proportion of convenience foods that require minimal preparation space?
☐ Would you like counters made from different materials to suit different cooking activities, such as a cool, smooth slab of marble for pastry-making? Or would you prefer the same surface material throughout the kitchen?
☐ Are you a sociable cook who prefers facing into the room while you work? Or do you prefer facing the wall, or looking out a window while you prepare food?

COOKING

Your preferred style of cooking – be it elaborate cuisine for entertaining, or quick reheating of convenience food, whether you are a solitary or sociable cook, how frequently you cook at home, and the number of people you regularly cook for – determines the type of cooking appliances.

☐ Do you want to face into the room while working at the stove? If so, consider a centrally placed cooking area.
☐ Would the type of cooking you enjoy benefit from an easy-to-control fuel, such as gas or convection?
☐ Would a wipe-clean ceramic stovetop make kitchen cleaning less of a chore?
☐ If you enjoy gourmet cooking, would you benefit from a stove fitted with extra features, such as a barbecue grill?
☐ Would a ventilation system be useful to help dispel cooking smells? If so, would a permanent or retractable hood be more suitable in the space above the stove?
☐ Do you regularly cook for more than five people? If so, is your oven big enough, or would a double oven or heavy-duty range be more suitable?
☐ Would you like to have the capacity to prepare, reheat, or defrost meals in an instant? If so, have you allowed space to accommodate a microwave oven?

EATING

Think carefully about the sort of meals that you would like to eat in the kitchen, whether just breakfasts and snacks, or lunches and suppers; the number of people that sit down to eat at any one time; and how often you entertain. These decisions will help you determine the size and type of table you need, plus the dimensions and best location of the dining area.

☐ Do you want to eat in the kitchen or would you rather eat in a separate room?
☐ What meals do you specifically want to eat in the kitchen?
☐ How many people do you want to be able to seat on a day-to-day basis?
☐ Do you want to entertain in the informal surroundings of the kitchen?
☐ Have you planned the location of the table so that it has a good source of natural light, is draft-free, and sits away from the main kitchen activity areas?
☐ Would a foldaway table or small corner table be more suitable if space is limited?
☐ Would a bar eating area around a central island be sufficient?
☐ Would a built-in window seat or banquette rather than chairs help you fit more seats around a table?
☐ Is a hard-wearing tabletop an important requirement?

DISHWASHING AND WASTE DISPOSAL

Make dishwashing and food recycling simple by choosing the sink, drainage space, and dishwasher on the basis of the amount of work you have to do.

■ DISHWASHING:
☐ If you use a large quantity of plates and glasses on a daily basis, is it worthwhile investing in a dishwasher to save time? If the dishwasher is going to be on while you are in the kitchen, have you checked that it has a quiet operational noise level?
☐ If you use many large pans, do you have a big enough sink to be able to wash them properly?
☐ While washing dishes, do you want to face the wall or have a window view, or perhaps face into the room?

■ WASTE:
☐ Will you dispose of all kitchen waste, or are you going to recycle some of it?
☐ Do you have the space in the kitchen to store recycling bins for items such as newspapers, bottles, and cans, or will they be stored outside, or in the garage?
☐ Would you like to store food waste for a compost heap? If so, have you a bin next to the preparation area for food scraps?

HOW THIS BOOK WORKS

THIS BOOK explains the practical know-how you need to design a room that matches your lifestyle and create an efficient and comfortable living space; it will help you plan a brand-new kitchen or adapt an existing one. A series of questions helps you assess what you want from your own kitchen; then, a survey of appliances and fittings guides you to elements that best suit those needs. Next, three-dimensional plans of six kitchens explain how to engineer a successful design, and finally, instructions on measuring and drawing up a kitchen plan leave you equipped to translate ideas into reality.

2. SELECT EQUIPMENT ▽

To help you compile a list of the features that will best suit your needs, a range of appliances and equipment are surveyed (*pp16–47*). A "Remember" box draws your attention to the key design points, and the pros and cons of each element are discussed. Where the height of a counter or an appliance may have some bearing on how easy it is to use, a small diagram recommends ideal dimensions and the most efficient height.

1. IDENTIFY YOUR NEEDS ▽

A number of preliminary questions (*pp12–13*) are asked to encourage you to think about your kitchen needs, and the condition and potential of your present kitchen. By examining aspects of your lifestyle that you take for granted, such as how you cook, eat, and wash dishes, you will find it easier to identify the best appliances and most appropriate design solutions for remodeling your kitchen or building a new one.

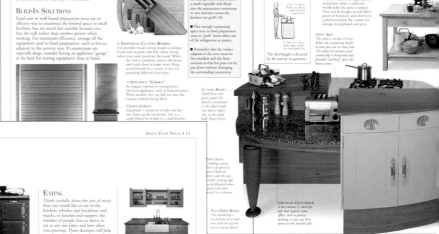

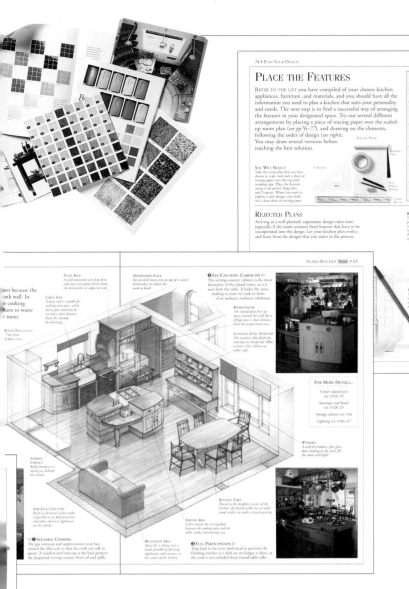

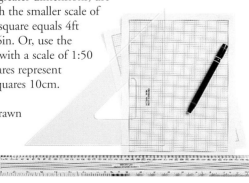

4. DESIGN YOUR KITCHEN △

When you feel satisfied with your own kitchen ideas, turn to *Plan Your Design* and put your design thoughts into practice (*pp74–81*). This section provides step-by-step instructions for measuring the room intended for your kitchen, plus details on how to draw the floor plan and different wall elevations to scale. Arriving at a solution takes time, so draw up variations on tracing paper, and pick out the best from each.

3. LEARN HOW TO PLAN △

A chapter on *Room Plans* (*pp48–73*) looks at six existing kitchen designs in detail and offers advice and inspiration on how to bring together all the elements in your own plan. A three-dimensional drawing, a bird's-eye-view plan, photographs, and a list of design points explain the thinking behind each design solution.

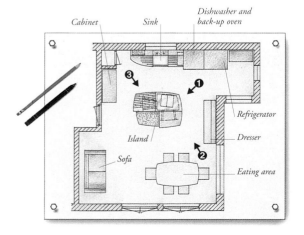

Cabinet Sink Dishwasher and back-up oven
Refrigerator
Island Dresser
Sofa
Eating area

HOW TO USE THE GRAPH PAPER

■ Draw up your room to scale (*see pp80–81*) using the graph paper provided (*pp89–96*). You may photocopy it if you need more.

■ For a room with small dimensions, use the graph paper with an imperial scale of 1:24, where one large square represents 1ft and a small square 3in. Alternatively, use the metric scale of 1:20, where one large square represents 1m and one small square represents 10cm. Therefore, an area 60cm long is drawn as six small squares.

■ For a room with greater dimensions, use the graph paper with the smaller scale of 1:48, where a large square equals 4ft and a small square 6in. Or, use the metric graph paper with a scale of 1:50 where the large squares represent 1m and the small squares 10cm.

■ With the room drawn on graph paper, try various designs on a tracing paper overlay.

KITCHEN ELEMENTS

FRESH FOOD STORAGE

IF YOU COOK with a lot of fresh produce, try to plan well-ventilated storage facilities set away from hot, steamy areas of the kitchen, rather than becoming totally dependent on the refrigerator. To avoid unnecessary waste and for a healthy turnover, ensure all fresh supplies are visible.

LARGE STORAGE

A specially designed cabinet is the modern-day answer to the walk-in pantry. Its generous storage capacity allows you to keep all your foods – with the exception of those that are kept in the refrigerator – in one location rather than at a variety of sites above and below the countertops. A successful pantry cabinet has shelves with adjustable heights to meet the demands of modern packaging, and a shallow depth so that items at the back do not disappear.

TOP SHELF
Less frequently used items, or those that you have bought in bulk, can be stored at this less accessible height, out of sight.

SHALLOW SHELVES
Avoid overfilling the door shelves with heavy items or they may be difficult to open.

MODERN LARDER △
A pantry cabinet with sliding, fold-back doors allows maximum visibility and accessibility, while requiring the minimum clearance when opening. Stainless-steel racking shelves allow air to circulate within; walls, floor, and doors are easy to clean.

PULL-OUT DRAWERS
Fresh vegetables, bread, or large goods can be placed in compartments below waist height.

PANTRY CABINET ▽

An attractive piece of furniture that stands away from the main traffic, this cabinet offers cool, dark, well-ventilated storage for a wealth of fresh and nonperishable produce. Half-depth shelves keep items in reach and prevent them from becoming lost and forgotten.

REMEMBER

■ Work out in advance which foods you prefer to keep in the pantry cabinet and which in the refrigerator. If you buy food in bulk, you will need additional storage areas.

■ When choosing a pantry cupboard, the central shelf should be about 24in (60cm) deep, while access to mid-height shelves is easiest if these shelves are 6–12in (15–30cm) shallower than the central shelf.

■ If you intend to store a lot of fresh produce in the cabinet, ventilation ducts to the outside may improve conditions. The pantry needs to be dark inside to slow down the deterioration of fresh fruit and vegetables.

FULL-HEIGHT DOORS
Doors of this size reveal the entire contents of the cabinet when open.

GRANITE SHELF
A cold granite shelf 24in (60cm) deep, keeps cheese and other fresh produce at room temperature.

SMALL STORAGE

Certain fresh foods, such as tomatoes, eggs, soft fruits, and baked foods, are damaged by cold refrigeration and taste best if kept at room temperature. Here are some modern and traditional solutions to this problem.

△ **BREAD-BOX DRAWER**
This space-saving alternative to a traditional bread-box has a lift-out drawer for removing crumbs. The wooden lid can double up as a cutting board.

REVOLVING RACK ▷
A modern rack provides dark, well-ventilated conditions to store root vegetables.

WIRE-MESH DOORS
These keep household dust and insects off fresh foods.

MEAT SAFE ▽
A traditional meat safe, with its netted doors, is practical for keeping flies off fresh food, while allowing ventilation; central heating and warm summers limit their use to eggs, cheeses, various soft fruits, and tomatoes.

RAISED HEIGHT
A meat safe on legs ensures that food is stored above floor level.

STORAGE HEIGHT

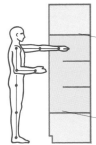

Ideally, the top shelf should sit at eye level.

Low shelves should be widely spaced or become drawers to house large items.

The most accessible storage area sits between knee height and eye level. Store items rarely used above and below this line.

CHILLED FOOD STORAGE

WHEN JUDGING WHICH refrigerator or freezer best suits your needs, bear in mind the size of your family, your shopping and eating habits, and the position the appliance will occupy in the kitchen. How you organize your food in the space available is the key, so check that the model of your choice has adjustable shelves and see-through drawers to offer the most flexibility.

DOOR SHELVES
Store short-term frozen items here, for easy access.

UNDERCOUNTER REFRIGERATOR/FREEZER

In a small kitchen, consider an undercounter, side-by-side refrigerator/freezer that will keep limited countertop space free for food preparation. If the appliance is flush-fitting, the interior space is well organized, and the appliance is placed directly below a food preparation area, it can work very efficiently. Bear in mind, though, that the refrigerator is one of the most-used items in the kitchen, and frequent bending down to take out food may become irritating.

SMALL REFRIGERATOR ▽
Think carefully before deciding to buy a small refrigerator. If you enjoy cooking on a regular basis, you may find its limited capacity very inconvenient.

REFRIGERATOR INTERIOR
Ensure the space inside allows for tall items, such as bottles.

REFRIGERATOR DRAWERS ▽
A recent innovation in cold food storage is refrigerators and freezers that are compact enough to fit into the space of a drawer. These allow chilled fresh produce to be stored at a number of sites around the kitchen.

EASY ACCESS
Large refrigerator doors can be difficult to open; single pull-out drawers offer easier access.

FRESH PRODUCE
This section varies between 32°F (0.5°C) and 37°F (3°C), with 50 percent humidity.

HIGH HUMIDITY
In this drawer, a relative humidity of up to 90 percent keeps fruit and vegetables fresh and crisp.

REMEMBER

■ Before choosing a chilled storage system, consider how often you prepare and freeze meals in advance. Or does your cooking focus on fresh foods?

■ Other features that may influence your decision are: CFC content, noise level, defrost capability, and energy efficiency rating.

■ When locating a refrigerator within the room, leave space for access. Specify which way you want the door to hinge, and plan a counter nearby for loading and unloading food.

■ After a shopping trip, beware of packing the refrigerator too tightly with food as it takes time to return to a cool temperature.

FREESTANDING MODELS

Designed to stand alone as a kitchen feature, these appliances are not limited by the need to fit within standard cabinetry. Many models sit on wheels and can be easily moved for servicing or to a new location.

DAIRY COMPARTMENT
A transparent lid protects the contents from taste and odor transfer.

◁△ **MODERN STYLE**
Handles the length of the door (*above*) make it easy for adults and children to open the large refrigerator, and gain access to the well-organized contents in easy-clean plastic and glass compartments (*left*).

SPILL-SAVER SHELVES
Raised shelf edges help to contain spills.

DEEP DOOR SPACE
Large items can be stored two-deep, while a high side prevents tall cartons from toppling out.

▽ **TRADITIONAL STYLE**
If you prefer your refrigerator to be unobtrusive, consider housing it within a cabinet. Vegetables that need good ventilation but not refrigeration can be stored in baskets below.

VENTILATION
Vents at the front enable the unit to have a coil-free back so that it can be fitted flush with the wall.

FRUIT DRAWER
Located in the coolest part of the refrigerator, see-through fruit and vegetable drawers allow you to see what needs replacing or throwing out.

NONPERISHABLE FOOD STORAGE

ORGANIZATION OF and access to pantry cabinet supplies is paramount, but because canned, bottled, and dried foods have fewer environmental needs than fresh foods and location-sensitive appliances, one option is to keep them in slim units and corner carousels that can fill up leftover spaces in the kitchen.

NARROW SOLUTIONS

In larger kitchens, tall, dual-sided pull-out cupboards are an efficient option because items at the back can be easily accessed. Make sure there is room on either side to reach into the pull-out, and that there is a mid-height "fence" to prevent articles from falling out. Place less regularly used, heavier items, on the bottom shelf.

EASY OPENING
A centrally placed handle distributes the weight, making the unit lighter to open, even when it is full.

CLEARANCE HEIGHT
Allow space between each shelf for the easy retrieval and return of taller items.

TALL BOTTLE STORAGE
Space for tall bottles is created by removing the penultimate shelf divider.

BOTTLE SAFETY
The rail holding bottles in place is thicker for these heavier items.

LAMINATE FINISH
Hard-wearing laminates are easy to clean and will withstand use.

DIRECT ACCESS
Drawer runners are an integral part of the fence rail, so that access to the shelves is uninterrupted.

CAPACITY
Each shelf is deep and wide enough to hold at least four large bottles.

◁ PULL-OUT STORAGE
The success of this pull-out store cabinet lies in its flexibility and ease of access. The door slides open and is nudged closed, while shelf heights and compartment sizes can be altered to suit a variety of nonperishable produce.

BOTTLE PULL-OUT △
A narrow, belowcounter pull-out is useful for cooking oils, vinegars, and cooking wine. It can be tucked into a narrow space adjacent to the stove, oven, or preparation area.

WALL UNITS

Wall-mounted cabinets and racks provide storage space over countertops. They can be useful for holding spices, oils, and wine, if placed within reach of the food preparation area. In small kitchens where space is at a premium, wall units may be the answer, but in order to function ergonomically they should be at eye level. This height can be a problem because the cabinet may block your view of the counter when working, and also pin your head and shoulders back. For this reason, try not to place cabinets above heavily used countertops or the sink.

TOP SHELF
Least important jars should be stored on high shelves.

SHELF DEPTH
The shelves should be between 6–12in (15–30cm) deep so that items are visible.

CHICKEN-WIRE DOOR
A fabric-backed wire door allows air to circulate while protecting food items from direct sunlight.

WALL FIXTURE
Ensure wall brackets are securely mounted as the unit is extremely heavy when full.

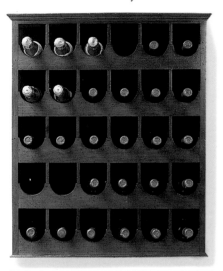

CONDIMENT CABINET ▷
Depending on how tall you are, place the cupboard at a height somewhere between 5ft 10in–7ft 2in (1.8–2.2m). Allow a gap of at least 18in (45cm) between wall units and the countertop below.

◁ WINE RACK
Consider storing your selection of wines on a wall rack to free up floor space. Do not position the rack too close to the oven because wine favors an even temperature around 60°F (15.5°C).

CORNER IDEAS

Even in very small kitchens where space is precious, the corner area where countertops meet is often neglected. This "dead" space can be turned into a useful storage area if a pull-out mechanism is fitted below counter level. Alternatively, plan a body-height carousel to fit neatly into a corner space, and bridge the gap that may be left between an eye-level oven and a food preparation counter.

OPEN CAROUSEL
Fixed doors revolve around a pivot and swing shut into place.

REAR SECTION
Once the front section has been pulled out, the rear section slides forward, out of the deep corner space.

◁ BODY-HEIGHT CAROUSEL
Rather than having to delve inside a dark corner cabinet, the doors of this unit fold back to offer access to its contents. Jars, cans, and packages are neatly arranged on four shelves that revolve when nudged. Standing 6ft 6in (2m) high, no effort is required to reach the top shelf.

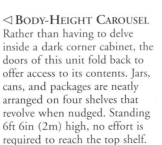

◁△ TWO-PART PULL-OUT
Contemporary kitchen manufacturers have responded to the challenge of kitchen storage needs by tailoring units to fit into awkward corners. In this two-part unit (*left and above*), frequently used nonperishable foods, such as pasta and noodles, sit in the front section (*left*), while items stored in bulk are kept at the back, and can only be accessed once the front unit has been swung to the side (*above*).

FOOD PREPARATION

TO ENSURE COOKING IS enjoyable, the chopping and preparation area needs ample space, a hard-wearing countertop, and clever positioning within the room; ensure food and equipment are close at hand, and that you can move with ease to the cooking zone and sink cabinet. To make the task more pleasant, plan an area where you have a view outside, natural light, or you can talk to family or friends.

BUILT-IN SOLUTIONS

Fixed unit or wall-based preparation areas are an effective way to maximize the limited space in small kitchens, but are much less sociable because you face the wall rather than another person when working. For maximum efficiency, arrange all the equipment used in food preparation, such as knives, adjacent to the activity area. If countertops are especially deep, consider having an appliance "garage" at the back for storing equipment close at hand.

REMEMBER

■ Chopping is the primary activity in food preparation. A good cutting surface is essential, so consider buying a built-in end-grain board – where the wood is turned on its end and glued together.

■ Arrange the preparation area so that you are close to the sink for rinsing fresh foods, or have a small vegetable sink fitted into the preparation countertop, to save journeys across the kitchen (see pp58–59).

■ Plan enough countertop space next to food preparation areas to "park" items taken out of the refrigerator or pantry.

■ Remember that the surface adjacent to the stove must be fire-retardant and also heat-resistant so that hot pans can be put down without damaging the surrounding countertop.

△ **INDIVIDUAL CUTTING BOARDS**
Use portable wood cutting boards to prepare foods such as garlic and fish, whose strong odors may easily penetrate the wood. When the task is complete, remove the board and scrub clean in soapy water. Keep several boards in a variety of sizes for preparing different food types.

◁ **APPLIANCE "GARAGE"**
An elegant solution to storing heavy electrical appliances, such as food processors. When needed, they are slid out onto the counter without being lifted.

CLOSED STORAGE
Equipment is stored out of sight and does not clutter up the countertop. This is a useful feature to include in a small kitchen.

▽ **MINI PREPARATION AREA**
A small food preparation center provides enough space to store knives, seasonings, and spices within easy reach of the activity area.

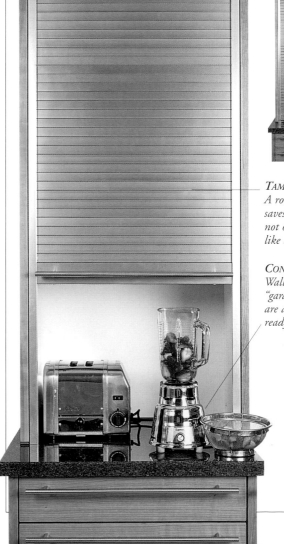

TAMBOUR SHUTTER
A roll-up mechanism saves space as it does not open outward like a cabinet door.

CONCEALED SOCKET
Wall sockets inside the "garage" mean appliances are always plugged in, ready for use.

VISIBLE STORAGE
Spices and pulses are attractively displayed in clear bottles and drawers for ease of use.

CUTTING BOARD
Made from end-grain wood, the board is positioned at the ideal height (see above right); slots in the wood hold sharp knives.

KNIFE SLOTS
A holding system that is designed to protect both the knives and the user; a knife's cutting edge can be blunted when stored with other utensils in a drawer.

PULL-DOWN BOARD
The countertop is saved from wear and tear with an easy-to-access cutting board.

FREESTANDING PREPARATION CENTERS

A central island unit or worktable provides a focus in the middle of the room dedicated to food preparation. These freestanding features (*right and below*) enable the cook to face into the space as he or she works and to join in the proceedings. In terms of kitchen planning, they provide a central focus, and a link with the features around the walls, especially in large kitchens. Islands should be placed so that they are within reach of stored food, the sink for rinsing ingredients, and the cooking zone.

HANGING RACK
Oils, garlic, and cooking utensils are stored within reach of the preparation area.

COUNTER HEIGHT

2–4in (5–10cm) below your flexed elbow for food preparation.

7–10in (17–25cm) below elbow-height for small appliances.

The ideal height is dictated by the activity in question.

LARGE WORKTABLE ▷
Wood worktables are appropriate in kitchens where a solid unit would make the space cramped. They can be bought as individual pieces of furniture, and often have a platform below the counter for storing mixing bowls and pans.

STOVE AREA
The stove is set 6in (15cm) below the countertop height so that you can see into pans. The adjacent stainless-steel countertop is heatproof and provides "parking" space for heavy items.

SERVING AREA
A free surface for resting plates of food, between the stove area and a kitchen table, makes serving easy. China and glass can be stored in the cabinet below.

LOW-LEVEL COUNTERTOP
A low counter is ideal for jobs that require some effort, such as pastry-making, as you can bear down on this marble slab.

◁ ISLAND UNIT
An island arrangement helps to concentrate key activities into a small area so the cook does not waste time and energy moving around the kitchen. The island is divided into zones for different activities. The activity determines the counter height, size, and also material for each zone.

FOOD RINSING AND GARBAGE DISPOSAL

HYGIENIC AND WELL-PLANNED food and waste management are essential to a well-run kitchen. Consider a sink with two basins, where fish, meat, vegetables, and fruit can be cleaned without interrupting other kitchen activities that require water, such as pan-filling. Plan convenient sites beneath food preparation centers for organic waste collection, and storage bins for collecting bottles and cans away from the main activity centers.

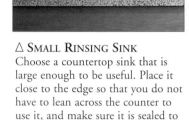

FOOD-RINSING SOLUTIONS

In large kitchens, where the distance between activity zones is greater, a second sink for washing food, close to the preparation area, may be convenient. Alternatively, plan a double sink unit, where food can be rinsed in one half and utensils, pans, and dishes washed in the other.

BACKSPLASH
A high stainless-steel guard protects the wall from water splashes.

△ **SMALL RINSING SINK**
Choose a countertop sink that is large enough to be useful. Place it close to the edge so that you do not have to lean across the counter to use it, and make sure it is sealed to prevent leakage into units below.

SPRAY-RINSING HEAD
An extendable spray attachment, for cleaning fresh ingredients, is linked to the water supply by a flexible hose.

◁ **DOUBLE SINK**
A double sink enables two people to stand at the sink at once and perform different tasks. Because the sink is used intensively, it is made from a durable water- and rust-resistant material, such as stainless steel.

DOUBLE BASIN
Use one sink to rinse fresh ingredients and the other to soak dirty pans and dishes.

FRONT PANEL
A stainless-steel panel prevents water from dripping onto the wood cabinet below.

MULTIPURPOSE SINK ▽
A well-designed, deep single sink can sometimes offer more flexibility than a double unit with two small sinks. A large sink can accommodate baking trays and pans, while a colander, draining rack, and cutting board can be slotted into the sink to divide up the internal space as required.

GARBAGE DISPOSAL
Flush food scraps washed off plates down into the garbage disposal unit fitted under the drain.

SINGLE FAUCET
Move the faucet to the left or right, depending on the task in hand.

COLANDER BASKET
Drain rinsed foods and t. replace the basket with th cutting board, stored belo

DRAIN RACK
Water drains directly into the sink. A separate plate rack or drainboard is no longer necessary.

TRASH RECYCLING

Households generate huge quantities of waste materials, much of which can be sorted out and stored for recycling. Before allocating space to recycling in your kitchen, contact the local authority to establish the categories of trash that they accept. If you have a garden, consider a compost heap.

ODOR-FREE BINS
Wash out bottles and cans before storage, or they will smell.

◁ **STACKING BINS**
Lightweight plastic bins can be easily stacked on top of one another, while lift-up flaps allow the quick deposit of items. Allocate one bin for each category of recycled waste. Store the bins out of sight and plan to empty them regularly.

△ **WET GARBAGE HOLE**
A hole or slot carved out of a wood counter feeds directly into a garbage can below, and is an efficient way of clearing away organic waste matter, like vegetable peelings. As well as keeping the counter free, the waste matter can be put directly onto a garden compost heap.

△ **RECYCLING COMPARTMENTS**
Here, a pull-out drawer adjacent to the sink holds two recycling cans. Avoid shallow pans that have to be emptied frequently. Make sure the pans are easy to lift out, and that the drawer interior can be wiped clean. Also, check that the drawer is sealed to prevent odor transfer.

REMEMBER

■ Plan organic garbage cans or a waste disposal hole close to the food preparation area to avoid having to carry food scraps across the kitchen.

■ The size of garbage cans for household waste needs to be in keeping with the size of your family. Emptying a can several times a day, especially if you live in an apartment block, may become annoying.

■ If you are unhappy about separating out waste materials for recycling, try to recycle just "clean" waste; newspapers and glass bottles are the easiest and cleanest to separate out and store in stacking bins for weekly recycling.

GARBAGE DISPOSAL

For those who live in apartments or small houses, recycling may not be an option because of the space needed to sort out and store the different materials. A trash compactor takes up a small amount of space and will compress bulky household trash into tight bundles. Consider a garbage disposal unit to dispose of food scraps, while the least expensive option is a slim, freestanding pedal can.

◁ **ELECTRIC COMPACTOR**
All household trash is fed in and then compacted at the turn of a switch. This small unit does not need emptying for several weeks at a time.

CHARCOAL FILTER
The filter reduces odors when the door is open.

PEDAL CAN ▷
A flexible unit that can be transported to wherever you are working. Its slim shape takes up less floor space than other pedal cans.

PLASTIC BOARD
This creates an extra cutting board above the sink. Organic waste can be swept directly into the garbage disposal unit.

GARBAGE-FREE SINK
Garbage does not interfere with sink drainage as it is fed directly into the garbage disposal system.

▽ **GARBAGE DISPOSAL UNITS**
If you do not intend to recycle organic waste, consider a sink fitted with an electric garbage disposer. This feature will grind food scraps and bones into a paste and then wash them away. It can be noisy when the grinder is switched on.

"PARKING" AREA
Place washed items here that are awaiting preparation.

BATCH FEED
The garbage disposal unit fits into this section. A safety plug is turned on to start up the electric grinder.

STOVES AND HOODS

THE POSITION AND CHOICE of stove is crucial to the enjoyment and efficiency of the kitchen. Ideally, it should face into the room, have a sink nearby, space suitable for resting hot pans, and, wherever possible, a high-performance, well-designed, powerful exhaust fan for removing cooking odors and steam. Lights built into the exhaust fan hood will light the stove area.

COMBINATION STOVES

A countertop-mounted gas, halogen, or induction stove and a wall-mounted electric oven offer flexibility of fuel types – quick response from the stovetop and even-temperature oven cooking. The variety of stoves has become increasingly specialized. Manufacturers now offer components such as steamers, griddles, or wok burners, so that you can build up stove features to suit your cooking style.

REMEMBER

■ In the life of your kitchen, much cooking time is spent standing at the stove. Arrange your kitchen plan accordingly by placing the stove in a safe, sociable, and convenient location, perhaps forming the central feature in an island arrangement (*see pp62–63*).

■ When planning a site for your stove, bear in mind the limitations of exhaust fans, required to expel steam and cooking smells. Fans work best when connected to outside walls; stoves on islands require more powerful systems.

■ US manufacturers usually rate their exhaust fans according to the amount of cubic feet per minute (CFM) of air they can process. Work out the volume of your room, to determine the rating you need.

■ A stove must be easy to clean to work efficiently. Many pan grids are now designed to fit into a dishwasher. Check that the rest of the stove is simply designed so that grease cannot collect in awkward corners.

■ Beware of unstable pan grids. If the prongs are short or stand high of the stove, saucepans may topple off the grid.

■ If your cooking habits demand constant use of the stove, ensure the stove floor and pan grids are made from heavy-duty materials; stainless steel and vitreous enamel are highly suitable.

GAS STOVE WITH GRIDDLE ▽
A solid, semiprofessional range can be fitted with a combination of different components that suit your cooking needs. Here, a powerful downdraft fan sits between a griddle and four gas rings.

GAS BURNERS
Cast-alloy pan grids surround the two gas burners.

PAN SPACE
A stainless-steel surface between the grids avoids overcrowding when four large pans are on the hob.

GRIDDLE PLATE
This flexible system enables food to be grilled on the stove rather than in an oven.

BUILT-IN FAN
Food odors and steam are sucked downward by an internal fan.

CONTROL KNOBS
Easy-grip, giant knobs make gas burners simple to control.

CERAMIC HALOGEN STOVE WITH STEAMER ▽
A ceramic stove flanked by two downdraft fans, a steamer, and a griddle, packs several distinct cooking functions into a small space. The hard-wearing granite countertop surrounding the burners can be used as a "parking" area for hot and heavy pans, and is fireproof.

COVERED GRIDDLE
A hinged lid can be pulled down when not in use to form a "parking" space for pans.

STEAMER WITH LID
If you enjoy steamed foods, this component saves valuable pan space on the stove.

CERAMIC STOVE
Fitted with halogen rings, this stove compares favorably in versatility to gas.

STOVE FAN
Fans on either side of the stove plate ensure steam and odors are quickly removed.

STOVES WITH HOODS

Condensation can be a problem in many kitchens as pans bubbling away on the stove produce both heat and moisture. To prevent this, and the peeling paint and mold that result, install a ventilation hood. If the hood has an internal, motorized fan, check that the motor runs quietly when on. If not, see whether the fan can be mounted on an outside wall. If you would rather not have a ventilation hood obstructing your headroom, consider a downdraft system (*bottom left*).

▽ **PROFESSIONAL GAS STOVE**
Many top-notch cooks favor gas stoves because they heat up quickly and the temperature is easy to control. Space can be wasted between four burners, but here, the area between pan grids holds two useful pan rests.

LOW-LEVEL STOVE ▷
Comparable to gas in flexibility, an induction stove only allows electric energy to be turned into heat inside the cooking pan, so that the stove surface remains at a safe temperature.

PULL-OUT HOOD
When several pans are on the go, pull out the visor; otherwise tuck it away to maintain clear headroom.

STAINLESS-STEEL SIDES
Raised edges improve safety and hygiene, by keeping hot food splashes within the stove area.

PAN STORAGE
Open shelves below the stove are convenient, but grease and dust soon collect on unused pans.

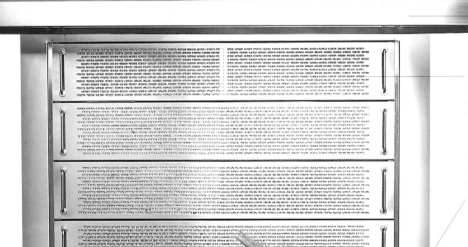

FAN HOOD
Ensure task lights are fitted under the hood to light up the stove area.

HOOD HEIGHT
The distance between hood and stove is crucial to the efficiency of the fan. Follow manufacturer's recommendations.

FAN GRILLE
Set against the wall, this system sucks in steam and fumes before they escape into the room.

GAS BURNERS
Unlike electric rings that eventually burn out, gas burners last indefinitely, and the flames are controllable.

STOVE HEIGHT

When cooking, you can see inside pans.

Stove sits 4–7in (10–17.5cm) below flexed elbow height.

Place the stove at a lower height than surrounding countertops, to protect the surfaces from fat splashes.

OVEN COOKING

TODAY'S COOK can choose from an extensive range of free-standing and built-in ovens with a choice of cooking options. Some, referred to as "semiprofessional," are heavy-duty ovens and resemble those used by restaurant chefs. Beware of being seduced by good looks and list your priorities, such as size, self-cleaning ability, and energy efficiency, before making a decision.

RANGES

Many manufacturers now produce all-in-one ranges with either single or double oven facilities. A great advantage of combined units is that cooking activities are focused in one part of the kitchen. But if you tend to roast or oven-bake food, you may find bending down to access the oven tiresome. If your kitchen is small, a single oven and stove unit is best, but check there is space for the oven door to open.

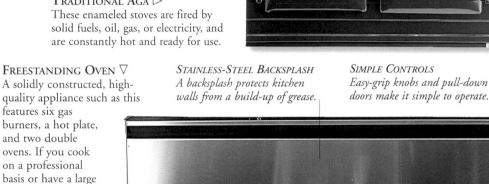

TRADITIONAL AGA ▷
These enameled stoves are fired by solid fuels, oil, gas, or electricity, and are constantly hot and ready for use.

FREESTANDING OVEN ▽
A solidly constructed, high-quality appliance such as this features six gas burners, a hot plate, and two double ovens. If you cook on a professional basis or have a large family, this oven may be a worthwhile investment.

STAINLESS-STEEL BACKSPLASH
A backsplash protects kitchen walls from a build-up of grease.

SIMPLE CONTROLS
Easy-grip knobs and pull-down doors make it simple to operate.

STAINLESS STEEL
A durable, brushed stainless-steel finish improves with age.

FLAT SIDES
The appliance can be fitted flush to cabinetry if you do not wish it to stand alone.

DOOR VENTILATION
Small vents keep these "child-height" doors cool on the outside.

SEE-THROUGH DOOR
A glass panel helps you check food without opening the door.

STORAGE DRAWER
Baking trays can be neatly stowed away when not in use.

FOUR LEGS
Short legs raise the oven off the ground so that the floor underneath can be swept.

△ SINGLE OVEN AND STOVE
A compact appliance for those without the space to house a separate oven at eye level. When switched off, the halogen stove doubles up as a countertop.

REMEMBER

■ Decide whether an oven at eye level is a priority. Bear in mind that a separate oven and stove, although convenient, may be more expensive.

■ If you want to use a powerful outdoor hood (*see pp28–29*), ensure that the oven and stove sit against an outside wall.

■ Check whether your floor is solid and can take the weight of a heavy stove.

■ If you wish to turn off your Aga during the summer, provide a back-up oven and stove.

EYE-LEVEL OVENS

Easier and safer to load than belowcounter ovens, an eye-level appliance has a simple pull-down oven door. The dish is placed inside without the extra effort of bending down, and you can watch your food as it cooks. If you enjoy catering for large numbers of people, a second oven for warming plates, grilling, or microwaving may be advantageous.

SLIDE-UP DOOR
One simple action raises the cabinet door that conceals the steamer.

STEAM OVEN
Although costly, consider this type of oven if it suits your eating habits.

OVEN HEIGHT

Dishes should not have to be lifted above chest height.

Place a single oven or two ovens housed in a tall unit, somewhere between eye level and waist height for ease of use.

SECOND OVEN
For maximum use, choose a fan-assisted model that can also grill and microwave.

SPACE BELOW
The ovens are fitted at the best height for the user, leaving space for a storage cabinet below.

STEAM OVEN COMBINATION ▷
For those who favor healthy, fat-free cooking techniques, a steam oven is the modern-day pressure cooker. By cooking food such as vegetables, rice, and fish in steam, the moisture is retained. Combine a steam oven with a multifunctional electric oven to cover all cooking options.

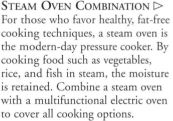

◁ DOUBLE OVENS
For keen cooks who enjoy baking, roasting, and grilling, a double oven combined with a separate stove is perhaps the answer. Opt for a solidly built appliance with easy-to-interpret controls and fold-down doors that serve as resting platforms for hot dishes entering or leaving the oven.

MICROWAVE AND OVEN ▷
For people with busy schedules, a microwave and electric oven may be the most useful combination. If cooking is really not your priority, install a dishwasher in the cabinet below the microwave instead of an oven, to save on time spent in the kitchen washing dishes (*see Family Kitchen Plan pp70–71*).

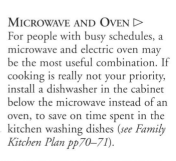

EATING

UNLESS YOU HAVE an exceptionally small kitchen, try to include an eating area in your plan because a table is the linchpin for a sociable kitchen. Above all, it is the gathering place where members of the family and friends naturally congregate. For this reason, the table should occupy the most comfortable space in the room, and have at its disposal the best source of natural light or a window view.

BUILT-IN TABLES

With careful planning, a small table where you can enjoy breakfast or a light supper can usually be accommodated in even the most compact of kitchens. It can also function as an extra work surface or a "parking" space for pans in transit.

FOLDING TABLE AND CHAIRS ▷
A folding kitchen table can offer an inexpensive solution for those who wish to eat in the kitchen but do not have the space for a permanent fixture. However, these tables can be unstable and make eating cramped.

FOLDING CHAIRS
Lightweight chairs can be folded away when not in use.

BREAKFAST BAR ▽
Wrapped around the cooking zone of an island stove, a granite breakfast bar offers a spacious, horseshoe-shaped table for informal meals.

TABLE SIZE
The table should have at least 12in (30cm) of space per place setting.

△ **AWKWARD-CORNER TABLE**
A custom-made triangular table makes imaginative use of an awkward corner. By creating a deep shape, there is enough room for two place settings to fit comfortably without cluttering the tabletop.

LAMINATE SURFACE
Ideal for messy children, this tabletop is easy to wipe clean but can scratch.

LOW-MAINTENANCE CHAIRS
Choose hard chairs that can be wiped clean rather than upholstered seating.

RAISED BAR HEIGHT
The counter is higher than the stove and hides any cooking mess from view.

LEG ROOM
A good folding design has space for uninterrupted leg room.

GRANITE TOP
A hard-wearing surface that does not burn or stain.

BAR STOOLS
For extra comfort, choose cushioned stools that support the back and have a footrest.

REMEMBER

■ The space allocated for a kitchen table is usually that which is left over once all the other fixtures and fittings have been placed. Try to keep the position of the table in mind when starting your design.

■ The aspect of the table is very important. Consider the best source of natural light and ensure the site is draft-free and warm, especially in winter.

■ Try to plan a cabinet near to the table for storing breakfast materials, table linen, china, glasses, cutlery, and any other table-setting equipment.

■ If you have children, the kitchen table becomes a center for homework, painting, and other tabletop activities. If you opt for a wooden kitchen table, choose one with an oiled rather than a lacquered finish as it will be more hard-wearing.

TABLE SHAPES

For people who do not have a formal dining room, or for those who simply prefer to eat in the relaxed atmosphere of the kitchen, the shape and size of the table are vital. Bear in mind that kitchen tables are usually round, oval, or rectangular, and each shape determines how people interact with one another. Table size is also worth considering because, although the room may be spacious, a large table may not be in keeping with the mood you wish to create, or how often you entertain.

ROUND TABLE ▷

Useful for filling a square kitchen floor area, small, round tables offer an intimate setting for four people, and are democratic as no one sits at the head. Large, round tables are less successful because of their wide diameter, which leaves guests raising their voices to be heard.

FOUR-SEATER TABLE
A table just over 3ft 3in (1m) in diameter seats four comfortably.

ELBOW ROOM

Each place setting is 12in (30cm) deep.

Allow a 22in (55cm) width of table space per person for eating without restriction, plus an extra 2in (5cm) on either side of each place, for chair movement without disruption.

OVAL TABLE ▽

An oval is perhaps the most successful shape for seating six people, as everyone can make eye contact. The generous center space stops the tabletop from becoming overcrowded.

RECTANGULAR TABLE ▽

For those who have a large family or who love to entertain, choose a large, rectangular table that seats up to 10 people. Here, eating is a communal activity, but of course a dining table of this scale needs a large kitchen.

INSET LEG
Slim legs allow space for two chairs at each end, to seat eight.

SEATING
If you want to save space taken up by separate chairs, build a banquette along one wall.

TABLE SIZE
This oval is 5ft 3in (1.6m) long x 4ft 3in (1.3m) wide at the center.

LONG TABLE
Over 6ft 6in (2m) long, the huge distance between ends can divide guests into two groups.

WASHING DISHES

THE DISHWASHING AREA is used more intensively than any other activity zone in the kitchen, so apply careful thought to its arrangement. There are several ergonomic aspects to resolve: the height of the sink; the depth of the washing bowl; the amount of space given over to draining; the proximity of china and cutlery storage; and the position of the sink cabinet to ensure an interesting viewpoint.

REMEMBER

■ Try to keep the distance between the sink, stove, and countertop areas to a minimum as preparation and cooking involves constant rinsing and cleaning of used utensils.

■ Consider the variety of tasks you wish to perform at the sink before deciding whether one large sink bowl or two or three smaller bowls would best suit your needs. Is the sink to be used solely for pans and oven trays, or for hand-washing china and glasses as well?

■ Arrange the sink cabinet so that there is enough space for drainboards on either side, and so that it has a pleasant aspect, perhaps a garden view.

■ If you intend to have a dishwasher, consider installing the appliance at a raised height, to avoid constant stooping down to load the machine.

WASHING BY HAND

Tailor your sink to your washing needs. If you cater to a large family on a regular basis, opt for a heavy-duty sink with long drainboards that is large enough for soaking big pots, oven pans, and cutting boards. A more compact unit will suit those who wash up one or two light meals a day.

TALL TOP SHELF
Although difficult to reach, less regularly used items can be kept here.

CHINA STORAGE
Glass-fronted cabinets and a plate rack provide storage within arm's reach.

DRAINBOARD
A wood surface provides more "give" so that fewer breakages occur.

SWAN-NECK FAUCET
Tall faucets with good clearance leave space for large pans.

SINK HEIGHT

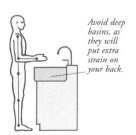

Avoid deep basins, as they will put extra strain on your back.

The ideal height for the top of the sink is 2in (5cm) below the base of a flexed elbow. The sink cabinet may be slightly higher than waist height but there will be no need to lean over.

PORCELAIN SINK △
This old-fashioned design has the advantage of being wide, deep, and also robust. It is installed without a frame, which means that the porcelain is visible and there is only a short distance to reach over into the sink. For it to function as a double sink for rinsing and washing, place a small plastic bowl inside the porcelain one.

WHITE PORCELAIN
Porcelain-coated fire clay offers a stain- and heat-resistant surface.

ANGLED DISHWASHING UNIT ▷
In a small kitchen, a wedge-shaped unit with a compact draining area contains this kitchen activity while freeing up space for other kitchen cabinets.

CAN LIGHTS
Built-in task lights above the sink provide a strong light and prevent a shadow from being cast over this area as you work.

COVERED RACK
Plates and cups drain directly into the sink and then, when dry, remain neatly stored behind a hinged door.

CLEANSERS
These are stowed on racks at eye level to keep the sink area uncluttered.

STAINLESS STEEL
Raised sides and a wide overhang prevent any water from overflowing onto the cabinet and floor below.

CURVED EDGE
For safety and good looks, the cabinet has a curved side rather than a sharp, angular edge.

DISHWASHERS

Research a number of products and compare reliability and life expectancy of the machines. Choose a model with valuable features, such as high energy efficiency, low operating noise levels, two revolving spray arms for a thorough wash, antiflood sensors, removable racks, and variable-sized plate and glass holders. Bear in mind that smaller, slimline models are available.

▽ COMBINED APPLIANCE

Small kitchens quickly become chaotic if dishes are left to pile up unwashed on counters. Make use of your sink plumbing to install a dishwasher underneath your sink unit at little extra cost.

GRANITE SURFACE
A hard-wearing granite countertop provides a stain-resistant surface.

INSIDE THE MACHINE
Stainless-steel interiors are more durable and less likely to stain and take on odors.

DOOR CLEARANCE
If the kitchen is narrow, make sure there is ample space to walk around the door when it is open.

HARDWARE STORAGE

USER-FRIENDLY CHINA, glass, and kitchen equipment storage relies on clever organization, so that items taken out on a regular basis are stored within reach – somewhere between knee height and eye level – and close to the activity area where they are needed. Much of this kitchenware is brought out, washed, and put back several times a day, so proximity to the sink or dishwasher also saves trips across the kitchen.

HIDDEN STORAGE

Kitchen hardware left out in the room on display and not used on a day-to-day basis soon gathers dust or becomes coated in a layer of grease. To avoid extra cleaning, or for those who prefer to keep countertops free of clutter, place items behind closed doors. Order the internal space so that frequently used equipment is near the front, and avoid storage systems with deep shelves.

LARGE BOWLS ON DISPLAY
Kitchen pieces add charm, but take them down regularly to clean.

SHELF DEPTH

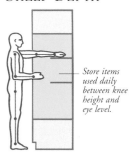

Store items used daily between knee height and eye level.

To avoid having to stretch, the ideal depth of shelving should not exceed 24in (60cm) to the back of the cabinet. Any deeper would be hard to reach.

COURT CUPBOARD ▷
A 19th-century Irish food cabinet with four doors and two drawers offers both an attractive and a practical storage facility. A large cabinet placed against a kitchen wall has a greater storage capacity than does a row of fitted base units and wall units in the same space.

CUPBOARD HEIGHT
The top shelf is within arm's reach, as the full height of the cupboard is only 6ft 2in (1.9m).

UTENSIL DRAWER
Store utensils in compartments to keep them sharp and in good condition.

△ **UTENSILS BELOW STOVE**
A shallow drawer, running below the stove, is divided up into nine front and nine back sections to keep small utensils in order. Each compartment has a curved base so that you can scoop out a utensil as it is required.

PAN DRAWER
A laminate finish ensures a hard-wearing interior.

△ **STORING PANS**
Like other kitchen hardware, pans should be stored close to the activity area. If you prefer your pans to be put away, one option is to install a deep drawer, below the stove, on strong runners that are fully extendable.

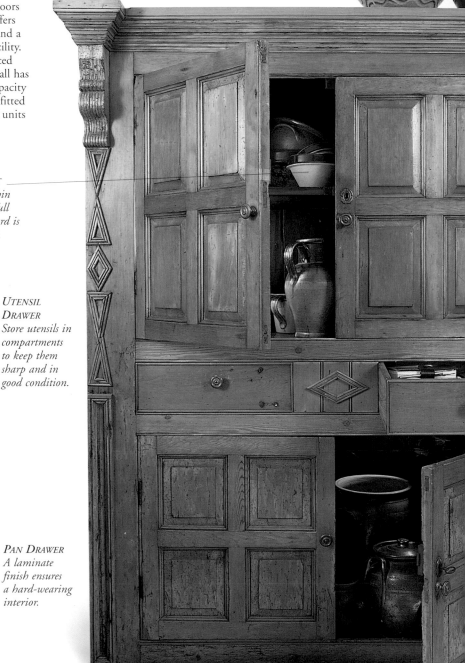

VISIBLE STORAGE

All kitchens gain in atmosphere when pots and pans, and other items associated with cooking and eating food, are on view. The most successful open storage systems, whether traditional or contemporary, are those where a sense of order prevails, and practical and aesthetic considerations are well balanced. For example, plates placed upright (*below*) not only look good but collect less dust on their surface.

SAUCEPAN TREE ▷
If an awkward corner exists close to your stove, a pan stand may be a useful storage feature, although take care, as tall stands can be slightly unstable.

PAN SIZE
Store progressively larger and heavier pans on lower levels.

◁ **TRADITIONAL DRESSER**
An antique dresser with its open shelves, hooks, drawers, and cupboards, provides a decorative but practical way to store and display cups, plates, cutlery, and glasses.

CUP HOOKS
Hang cups on the front edge of the shelves so that they do not take up valuable shelf space.

CABINET SPACE
Store less decorative, utilitarian items on shelves behind doors.

CARVED CABINET
Traditional features make the kitchen feel well-furnished, like other rooms.

DOOR WIDTH
Approximately 24in (60cm) wide, the doors are not too obtrusive when open.

DRAWER SPACE
House cutlery, table mats, instruction leaflets, and cut-out recipes in these generous drawers.

DUST-FREE STORAGE
China kept behind closed doors is less susceptible to dust and grease-laden kitchen fumes.

INDIVIDUAL COMPARTMENTS
A separate display space allocated to each item enhances the sense of order.

▽ **OPEN-FRONTED AND GLASS UNIT**
A built-in full-height system for those who like to be able to display decorative pottery and store utilitarian items in the same unit. Fit the cabinet on a wall linking cooking and eating areas.

PULL-OUT DRAWER
Translucent glass removes the tyranny of maintaining a neat display.

SLIDING GLASS DOOR
A good compromise, for even when the door is shut you can quickly locate items.

COUNTERTOPS

IN WELL-DESIGNED kitchens, individual countertops are built from different materials that change from one activity zone to the next. The choice of material is determined by the task undertaken as there is no one surface that can withstand scratches, stains, and heat marks, and be hard-wearing, easy to clean, and attractive. Compare the merits of each surface before choosing.

POINTS TO CONSIDER

■ Cover the area surrounding the stove with terrazzo, granite, or stainless steel. All three are heatproof, hard-wearing, and require little effort to maintain. If you are not planning to stay in your property for long, the cost of these materials may be a drawback.

■ For drainboards, the most appropriate materials are water-resistant, and provide a soft landing for delicate china and glassware that have to be washed by hand. Stainless steel, oiled hardwood, colorcore-type, and corian-type are all suitable.

■ Chopping and food preparation is best performed on wood. Consider buying a series of different-sized boards to lay on top of any surface, or install a slab of end-grain wood. Once regarded as a breeding ground for bacteria, wood is now known to be hygienic.

■ Granite and slate are both suitable surfaces for pastry-making because they are cool and smooth, and so preventing pastry from sticking.

■ Oiled hardwoods make attractive and easy to restore general surfaces, when away from heat.

STAINLESS STEEL

A near-perfect countertop material, used in professional kitchens where durability is important. A brushed finish is best.

ADVANTAGES
• A noncorrosive and heatproof material.
• Wipes clean easily and is very hygienic.
• Brushed stainless steel wears particularly well.

DISADVANTAGES
• Highly polished surfaces scratch easily.
• A noisy surface to work on.
• Difficult to fabricate into curved shapes.

GRANITE

A natural material available in a huge range of colors and patterns. It is cut to size and polished to make countertops.

ADVANTAGES
• Natural beauty does not deteriorate with age.
• Almost impossible to scratch or chip.
• Heatproof, waterproof, and difficult to stain.

DISADVANTAGES
• Expensive as it is a hard stone to machine-cut.
• Weight requires base cabinets to be strong.
• Dark colors can appear cold and murky.

SLATE

Many slates are too porous for kitchen use, but a few newly available types have a high silica content that reduces porosity.

ADVANTAGES
• Smooth surface is cool and pleasant to touch.
• Relatively hard-wearing if silica content is high.
• A cheaper alternative to granite and marble.

DISADVANTAGES
• Porous types of slate absorb oil and stain easily.
• A finish must be applied to reduce porosity.
• Colors can be dull and uninteresting.

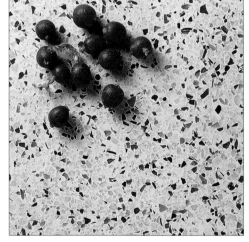

TERRAZZO

A lesser-known material, made from a mixture of marble and granite chippings set in white cement, and then polished.

ADVANTAGES
• Comes in wide variety of colors and patterns.
• Can be made up to your exact specification.
• Hard-wearing and waterproof.

DISADVANTAGES
• Costly and time-consuming to install.
• Not as hard-wearing as natural stones.
• Bolder patterns may lose their appeal in time.

LACQUERED HARDWOOD

The beauty of wood makes it a popular choice. These counters are coated with lacquer, above and below, for protection.

ADVANTAGES
- Wide range of different colors and grains exist.
- Counters match the wood cabinet finishes.
- Reasonably priced.

DISADVANTAGES
- Liquid spillages eventually dissolve the lacquer.
- Knife cuts permanently damage the surface.
- Not as hard-wearing as other wood finishes.

END-GRAIN WOOD

As its name suggests, this is wood turned on its end and glued together in blocks. It provides the best surface for cutting.

ADVANTAGES
- Very dense and wears evenly across the grain.
- Knife blades do not damage the end-grain.
- Blade is gripped on contact, making it safer.

DISADVANTAGES
- Central heating may cause the counter to warp.
- Absorbs strong food flavors, such as garlic.
- Wood may contract in centrally heated homes.

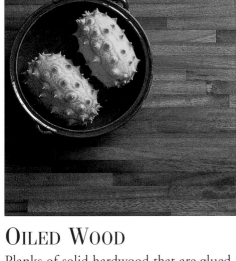

OILED WOOD

Planks of solid hardwood that are glued together and brushed with linseed oil to prevent the wood from splitting.

ADVANTAGES
- More resistant to heat than lacquered wood.
- Flexible surface that can withstand knocks.
- Sanding and a coat of oil restores its beauty.

DISADVANTAGES
- Central heating may cause it to warp or crack.
- Chopping on this surface leaves deep incisions.
- Some oiled hardwoods are expensive.

LAMINATE

A man-made material that has a paper center and is built up with thick coats of lacquer to create a flexible sheet material.

ADVANTAGES
- Huge choice of bright colors and patterns.
- Waterproof and easy to wipe clean.
- Simple and inexpensive to manufacture.

DISADVANTAGES
- Cutting directly onto the surface causes damage.
- In time, the laminate can deteriorate.
- Once damaged, the counter cannot be repaired.

COLORCORE-TYPE

This material is made from layer upon layer of colored paper, coated in a tough melamine-formaldehyde resin.

ADVANTAGES
- Knife cuts on counters can be sanded away.
- Subtle range of colors is available.
- Waterproof and simple to wipe clean.

DISADVANTAGES
- More expensive than laminate.
- Can become unstuck at the edges.
- Surface has no light-reflective qualities.

CORIAN-TYPE

A synthetic resin best installed in heavily used areas, such as around sinks, where it can be seamlessly joined to counters.

ADVANTAGES
- Rounded front edges are safer for small children.
- Joins between different sections are invisible.
- Sinks and counters are made from one piece.

DISADVANTAGES
- Difficult to install without professional help.
- Over long periods, paler colors may yellow.
- Can be as expensive as granite.

CABINET FINISHES

WHEN YOU HAVE DECIDED what cabinetry you would like in your new kitchen, consider the finish. Although this may seem a minor decorative detail, the choice of materials presents a major opportunity to influence the atmosphere of the room. Bear in mind that different surface finishes affect the quality of light. High-gloss or shiny finishes increase reflections and glare, while matte finishes are kinder on the eyes and diffuse light. Pale-colored units will brighten up dark kitchens, as will glass cabinets, while dark wood and dark synthetic finishes absorb light.

COMBINATION OF FINISHES
This adventurous design contrasts cherry wood with deep blue sprayed lacquer.

GLASS

Glass wall cabinets are useful in small kitchens, where they open up the space, and display decorative kitchen items.

ADVANTAGES
• Surface is easy to wipe clean with a soft cloth.
• Stored items are visible so are easy to find.
• Light-reflective quality brightens up dark rooms.

DISADVANTAGES
• Smudges of grease and dirt show on glass.
• Only neat, attractive items can be stored.
• Susceptible to knocks and may crack.

STAINLESS STEEL

Offering a durable metal finish that does not tarnish or rust, this surface works well near sinks and cooking areas.

ADVANTAGES
• Attractive surface sheen reflects light.
• Contrasts well with wood and painted surfaces.
• Matches appliances finished in stainless steel.

DISADVANTAGES
• Finger marks and water marks show up easily.
• Easy to scratch, especially polished finishes.
• Too much stainless steel looks clinical.

POINTS TO CONSIDER

■ When you have finalized your room plan, choose the finish for the cabinets at the same time as flooring, wall coverings, lighting, and counters – the interior design scheme.

■ The balance of colors and finishes is important. Too much of any one finish is overpowering and some, such as high-gloss polyester and brightly colored lacquers, are particularly overwhelming. These should be used only in small quantities, offset by natural materials like wood.

■ Ask yourself whether the kitchen design can be enhanced by using a combination of cabinet finishes to distinguish the key activity areas in the room.

■ List your favorite finishes in order of preference. Calculate how much each finish will cost to see what is affordable within your budget. Limiting expensive finishes to a few key areas and combining them with other materials will help to keep costs down.

■ Select hard-wearing materials for cabinets in intensively used areas and, if kitchen traffic is heavy or you have children, select the most durable finishes for base units.

■ If you cannot afford to install new kitchen cabinets, give the existing units a facelift simply by replacing or painting the cabinet doors and changing the style of handles to suit your taste.

WOOD VENEER

High-quality woods are often sliced into veneers, so for those who favor a wood kitchen, veneers can offer the best finish.

ADVANTAGES
• Color and texture are easy to live with.
• Grain configuration is better than solid wood.
• Unlike solid wood finishes, veneer does not warp.

DISADVANTAGES
• If moisture seeps in, the veneer may peel.
• Uniform tone and color may be monotonous.
• High-quality veneers can be expensive.

HAND-PAINTED WOOD

In contrast to smooth, synthetic finishes, these cabinets are painted by hand and can be "distressed" to add extra character.

ADVANTAGES
• Can select precise color to match your scheme.
• Damaged units can be repaired by repainting.
• Variability of finish between units adds charm.

DISADVANTAGES
• Needs several coats of varnish to protect it.
• Not as durable as other cabinet finishes.
• May need repainting in time.

CHICKEN WIRE

An unusual cabinet finish that appears purely decorative; however, stored items are kept well ventilated and dust free.

ADVANTAGES
• Enables air to circulate inside.
• Decorative effect with "country style" appeal.
• Inexpensive; easy to build without expert help.

DISADVANTAGES
• Dust may gather on fabric, making it unhygienic.
• Appearance limits it to one style of kitchen.
• Can stretch and distort.

POLYESTER

Offered by only a few manufacturers, this synthetic resin is sprayed thickly onto the cabinet for a high-gloss finish.

ADVANTAGES
• Smooth, high-gloss finishes are available.
• Hard-wearing finish is easy to wipe clean.
• Available in a huge range of bold colors.

DISADVANTAGES
• Glossy surface shows up greasy finger marks.
• More expensive than other synthetic finishes.
• High-gloss finish may cause kitchen glare.

LAMINATE

An economical plastic sheet material made from melamine, which is then glued onto a cabinet panel.

ADVANTAGES
• Both color and pattern are unlimited.
• More economical than other synthetic finishes.
• Can withstand knocks.

DISADVANTAGES
• If scratched, the finish cannot be repaired.
• Reflects light poorly and looks artificial.
• Laminates can lift at the corners if damp.

SPRAYED LACQUER

A clear lacquer is spray-painted onto the outside of a stained or painted cabinet to provide a protective finish.

ADVANTAGES
• Hard-wearing protective finish.
• Easy to wipe clean.
• Less expensive than a polyester finish.

DISADVANTAGES
• Impossible to repair on site.
• Finish can look flat and lackluster.
• More expensive than a laminate finish.

WALL COVERINGS

SELECTING A WALL finish for your new kitchen is not simply a style issue. The kitchen is often the most-used room in the home, and hot and steamy conditions put special demands even on the walls. The wall areas that take the most abuse are those behind the sink, stove, oven, and food preparation countertops. Stray splashes soon spoil wallpaper or paint, so install a guard made from an easy-wipe material. It is details such as these that will help you create not just a kitchen with character but one that is a pleasure to work in.

PROTECTIVE WALL FINISH
The cooking range sits in an alcove that has been tiled to provide an easy-clean surface.

POINTS TO CONSIDER

■ When you have chosen countertops and cabinetry, think about the walls. Consider wall coverings that either match or contrast with the cabinet finishes. Pay particular attention to the wall area between the counter and the wall cabinets, known as the backsplash.

■ Try choosing a backsplash that contrasts with the dominant material. For example, natural wood cabinetry looks good with a dark granite backsplash.

■ For the backsplash behind the stove, choose a heat-resistant material, such as stainless steel, ceramic tile, or natural stone.

■ If you decide to paint the walls, choose oil-based or gloss paint finishes that are durable and can be washed down. Avoid latex paints, especially if ventilation is poor, because they do not stand up so well to condensation.

■ If the kitchen has a high percentage of plastic finishes, use natural materials, such as wood paneling, to redress the balance.

■ If the room is north-facing or has a low ceiling, use paler colors on the walls to reflect light from windows, and to create a feeling of space. A backsplash of etched glass will help to reflect light onto counters.

KITCHEN WALLS

PLASTER WALLS

Once a technique for preparing walls, bare plaster is now a popular wall finish and comes rough, polished, or stained.

ADVANTAGES
• Masks uneven walls, turning them into a feature.
• Durable and inexpensive finish.
• Provides an opportunity to add character.

DISADVANTAGES
• Rough plaster attracts dust and is hard to clean.
• Can look artificial if not well rendered.
• Requires a backsplash around countertops.

BACKSPLASHES

DECORATIVE GLASS

Rarely used in kitchens, the waterproof and heat-resistant properties of glass make it a good choice for backsplashes.

ADVANTAGES
• Useful around sink areas and cooking zones.
• Easy to wipe clean.
• Reflects light, and introduces a decorative finish.

DISADVANTAGES
• Difficult to transport to site and install.
• May break if struck with a hard object.
• Expensive as specially cut from templates to fit.

OIL-BASED PAINT

The most versatile kitchen wall covering, oil-based paints with durable finishes, such as eggshell and gloss, are best.

ADVANTAGES
- Wide range of colors with durable finishes.
- Walls can be wiped clean with a sponge.
- Simple to retouch small areas or repaint room.

DISADVANTAGES
- Not tough enough to be used as a backsplash.
- Gloss paints show up imperfections in walls.
- Painted walls may peel or become mildewed.

WASHABLE WALLPAPER

Plastic-coated, wipe-clean wallpapers are practical, especially if you have very small children, but color choice is limited.

ADVANTAGES
- Waterproof plastic surface is easy to wipe clean.
- Can be put up after cabinetry is installed.
- Inexpensive; covers up uneven plasterwork.

DISADVANTAGES
- Steam may cause wallpaper to peel.
- Plastic "sheen" on surface can look artificial.
- Impossible to repair small area once damaged.

WOOD PANELING

Useful for covering up uneven areas on walls and ceilings, painted wood panels will also help insulate heat and sound.

ADVANTAGES
- Easy to install without expert help.
- Hides irregular walls or uneven plasterwork.
- Absorbs kitchen noise.

DISADVANTAGES
- Good quality paneling not always available.
- Unsuitable material for sink and cooking area.
- Traditional look does not suit all kitchen styles.

MANUFACTURED TILES

Less expensive than handmade tiles, these are ideal for tiling large wall areas, perhaps behind an oven or a sink.

ADVANTAGES
- Easy-to-clean flat surface and thin grouting.
- Heat resistant, so suitable for cooking areas.
- Pale tiles covering large areas look inoffensive.

DISADVANTAGES
- Regular shape and surface can look boring.
- Can detract from character of room.
- Darker colored tiles can be less hard-wearing.

HANDMADE TILES

Available in a vivid range of colors and finishes, these hard-wearing tiles offer great decorative possibilities in kitchens.

ADVANTAGES
- Handmade quality adds character to kitchen.
- Wide range of colors, finishes, and sizes.
- Hard-wearing and waterproof.

DISADVANTAGES
- Uneven shape tiles require thicker grouting.
- Grouting collects dirt and takes time to clean.
- Patterned tiles can become difficult to live with.

GRANITE

This popular kitchen material is often used as a backsplash above granite counters. It works best in small areas.

ADVANTAGES
- Hard-wearing and low-maintenance.
- Easy to clean, with few grouted seams.
- Continuity; it can match a granite counter.

DISADVANTAGES
- Dark, cold appearance unsuitable for large areas.
- Complicated to fit around plug sockets.
- Expensive; has to be cut off-site, to a template.

FLOORINGS

CHOOSING THE RIGHT material for your new kitchen floor needs careful thought. It is a delicate balancing act between finding a hard-wearing, hygienic material, aesthetic preferences, and cost. Wooden floors are warm, easy to sweep clean, and good value but long-term durability and water-resistance around the sink unit are a problem; limestone and slate are hard-wearing but can be cold and hard on the feet. Modern materials, such as vinyl, are also appealing because, although they are not as long-lasting as natural materials, they are lower in cost and easier to replace when worn.

WOOD

The warmth of color, choice of grains, and "give" underfoot make natural wood popular, but it must be well sealed.

ADVANTAGES
• Reasonably priced and straightforward to install.
• China often "bounces" when dropped on wood.
• It complements wood cabinetry and counters.

DISADVANTAGES
• Few protective finishes last, especially when wet.
• Too much wood in one room is overpowering.
• Requires regular maintenance.

VARNISHED WOOD FLOORING
A strip-pine floor complements the simplicity of this painted wood kitchen.

LIMESTONE TILES

Enthusiasm for this natural stone means that quarried limestone is easy to obtain. Choose one with a low level of porosity.

ADVANTAGES
• A wide choice of colors, textures, and patterns.
• Durable and low maintenance if properly sealed.
• Resistant to heat, water, and household solvents.

DISADVANTAGES
• Some porous types need several coats of sealant.
• Hard surface is cold on the feet and noisy.
• Lighter colors show up dirt easily.

POINTS TO CONSIDER

■ Think carefully about your selection of materials for cabinet finishes, countertops, appliances, and soft furnishings before making a final decision on flooring. This way, you can ensure that all the elements in the kitchen complement one another. Do not forget to look at the floor in the hall or adjacent rooms; too many changes of finish from one room to the next in a small house can appear fussy and tiresome.

■ Bear in mind the cost of laying the floor as well as the purchase price of materials. All floors, except vinyl and linoleum, should be laid before cabinetry and appliances are installed. Ensure the new floor is well protected during other installations.

■ The amount of day-to-day maintenance you are willing to undertake may influence your floor choice. Some materials, such as wood, require more care, especially around the sink, where water damages the varnish.

■ Decide whether the kitchen is large enough to accommodate two floor finishes. You may prefer limestone tiles around the cooking zone, where activity is concentrated, and wood flooring in the eating area.

■ If you choose tiled flooring, bear in mind that large rooms need large, plain tiles; small, patterned tiles will look too busy. Flagstones and large terra-cotta tiles suit the scale of huge family kitchens.

GLAZED CERAMIC TILES

The most hard-wearing and impermeable of all flooring materials, glazed ceramic tiles do not need sealing for protection.

ADVANTAGES
• Low maintenance and almost indestructible.
• Mass-produced, so easy and inexpensive to buy.
• Available in a huge range of bold colors.

DISADVANTAGES
• Hard on feet and slippery when wet.
• Grout between tiles can be difficult to clean.
• Strong-colored glazes can be overpowering.

TERRA-COTTA TILES

Brand-new and reclaimed terra-cotta tiles are available. In time, new tiles develop the rich patina common to old ones.

ADVANTAGES
• Clay is warmer than stone underfoot.
• Variety of colors, textures, shapes, and sizes.
• Sealed tiles are water and stain resistant.

DISADVANTAGES
• Unsealed tiles are porous and stain easily.
• Difficult to find matching old tiles in quantity.
• High-quality tiles can be expensive.

SLATE

Popular because of its natural variations in color from gray to green and purple, slate is precision-cut into sheets or tiles.

ADVANTAGES
• Wide range of colors and sizes available.
• Choice of smooth or rough natural finishes.
• Wears well over the years and is waterproof.

DISADVANTAGES
• Large pieces are brittle and may crack or peel.
• Hard and cold underfoot.
• Large sheets are expensive.

CORK TILES

Manufactured by compressing cork, this flooring is inexpensive but rather dull in comparison to other natural floorings.

ADVANTAGES
• Warm and soft underfoot, and extremely quiet.
• Inexpensive and easy to lay without expert help.
• Sealed cork tiles are stain resistant.

DISADVANTAGES
• Color, texture, and pattern are uniform and dull.
• Tiles are only stuck down with glue so may lift.
• Tiles damaged by water will need replacing.

VINYL

A cheap, flexible plastic that is produced in sheet or tile form. It is available in a huge range of colors and patterns.

ADVANTAGES
• Soft and quiet underfoot, and nonslip.
• Inexpensive and easy to lay on a flat surface.
• Hard-wearing and waterproof.

DISADVANTAGES
• Tends to discolor with age.
• Reflects light poorly and looks artificial.
• Ripples may form if laid on an uneven floor.

LINOLEUM

Produced from natural ingredients, such as linseed oil, linoleum comes in sheets or is hand-cut for intricate patterning.

ADVANTAGES
• A quiet, warm surface that cushions your feet.
• Manufactured from all-natural substances.
• Durable and low-maintenance.

DISADVANTAGES
• More costly than vinyl and needs expert fitting.
• Water can seep under unsealed edges.
• It may scuff or mark if not kept well polished.

LIGHTING

A WELL-DESIGNED lighting system is a vital ingredient for achieving a pleasant working and eating environment in the kitchen. As electrical fittings have to be installed well before cabinetry and appliances, decide at an early stage in your kitchen design where in the room directional task lights or softer ambient lighting are needed. The exact position of the fittings is also important; if they are installed too far back from the wall units, you will always be standing in front of the light source and casting a shadow over your work.

MULTIPURPOSE LIGHTING SYSTEM
Track lights link kitchen and eating areas; undercabinet lights illuminate the counters.

POINTS TO CONSIDER

■ Low-voltage lights have two main advantages. They use 30 percent less electricity than ordinary bulbs and are much smaller, but they do require a transformer to make them compatible with the household electricity. Some low-voltage lights have built-in transformers, but others have a separate element that needs to be hidden. Consult an expert.

■ Check what material your kitchen ceiling is made from because you will not be able to fit recessed can lights into concrete. To solve this, you will need to build a false lower ceiling out of plasterboard. Ask a specialist if you are unsure.

■ You will need to plan a minimum of two electrical circuits for a small kitchen, one for task lights and one for general lighting, and up to five circuits for a large room: one to two circuits for counters, the front of cabinets, and the table; one floor lamp circuit for the ceiling; and one circuit to light a sitting area, plus an extra booster circuit to light lesser areas.

■ Ask an electrician to check whether your fusebox can cope with your lighting needs, whether the circuits are shared with other rooms, and whether the lights can be routed to work with other electrical appliances. Ask for an estimate to help plan your budget.

TASK LIGHT

CAN LIGHTS

Low-voltage can lights are discreet. Place them 3ft 3in (1m) apart, and about 12in (30cm) from the wall to avoid shadows.

ADVANTAGES
• Strong, directional light spotlights countertop.
• Recessed fitting is protected and free from dust.
• Reduced glare when viewed from a distance.

DISADVANTAGES
• Wall-mounted units can block the light cast.
• The angle of the light can be difficult to adjust.
• Bulbs in some fittings can be hard to remove.

ATMOSPHERIC LIGHT

STANDARD FLOOR LAMP

Designed for eating or relaxation areas in larger kitchens, this freestanding light is operated on a dimmer switch.

ADVANTAGES
• Flexible; it can be moved around where needed.
• Boosts light in dark, forgotten corners.
• Light never shines directly into your eyes.

DISADVANTAGES
• Needs to be positioned near a wall socket.
• Unsuitable for small areas as takes up floor space.
• Away from the source, the light is cold and weak.

UNDERCABINET LIGHT

Used to light shadowy areas under wall-mounted units, a fluorescent tube is hidden behind a length of cabinet trim.

ADVANTAGES
- Lights up potentially dark areas on counters.
- Cheaper to install than halogen can lights.
- Solves the problem of working in your shadow.

DISADVANTAGES
- Fluorescent tubes cast a harsh, clinical light.
- In time, fluorescent tubes may start to "hum."
- Brightness focuses attention on the counters.

TRACK LIGHTS

Wall- and ceiling-mounted tracks offer flexible lighting, but the lamps become hot and must be out of a child's reach.

ADVANTAGES
- Tracks are low cost and easy to install.
- Flexible; as lamps are multidirectional.
- Task lights can be placed on walls and ceilings.

DISADVANTAGES
- Generate considerable heat and burn if touched.
- Exposed lamps collect dust and are hard to clean.
- Can cause eye-burn if stared at for too long.

CLIP-ON SPOTLIGHT

A temporary solution for unexpected lighting demands, the light cast is limited and cables can get in the way.

ADVANTAGES
- Inexpensive to buy and no installation costs.
- Task light directed exactly where you want it.
- Simple fittings are often well designed.

DISADVANTAGES
- Cables can obstruct other kitchen activities.
- Uses sockets needed for electrical appliances.
- Needs to be clipped onto a suitable feature.

WALL UPLIGHTS

Suitable for high-ceilinged rooms, they cast an atmospheric light when placed 12–24in (30–60cm) from the ceiling.

ADVANTAGES
- Cheap to install if have same household voltage.
- Fills wall space in "low-demand" area near ceiling.
- Creates a different mood for kitchen eating.

DISADVANTAGES
- Works only as a secondary light source.
- Inappropriate for rooms with low ceilings.
- May need a high-wattage lamp on a dimmer.

PENDANT TABLE LIGHT

Hanging above the kitchen table, a pendant light creates a separate lighting environment for informal dining.

ADVANTAGES
- Creates a strong identity for the table area.
- All other lights can be switched off when eating.
- Lowers the ceiling to create an intimate space.

DISADVANTAGES
- Table position in kitchen has to stay fixed.
- People may hit their heads as they sit down.
- Works best with round or square-shaped tables.

CANDLELIGHT

If you do not have a dining room, use candles to transform a meal in the kitchen into a special occasion.

ADVANTAGES
- Softens a harsh kitchen environment.
- Makes dining in the kitchen an event.
- Disguises half-tidy counters and cooking areas.

DISADVANTAGES
- Trips to the stove at mid-meal can be difficult.
- Several candles are needed to see food properly.
- Smoke from candles may trigger a smoke alarm.

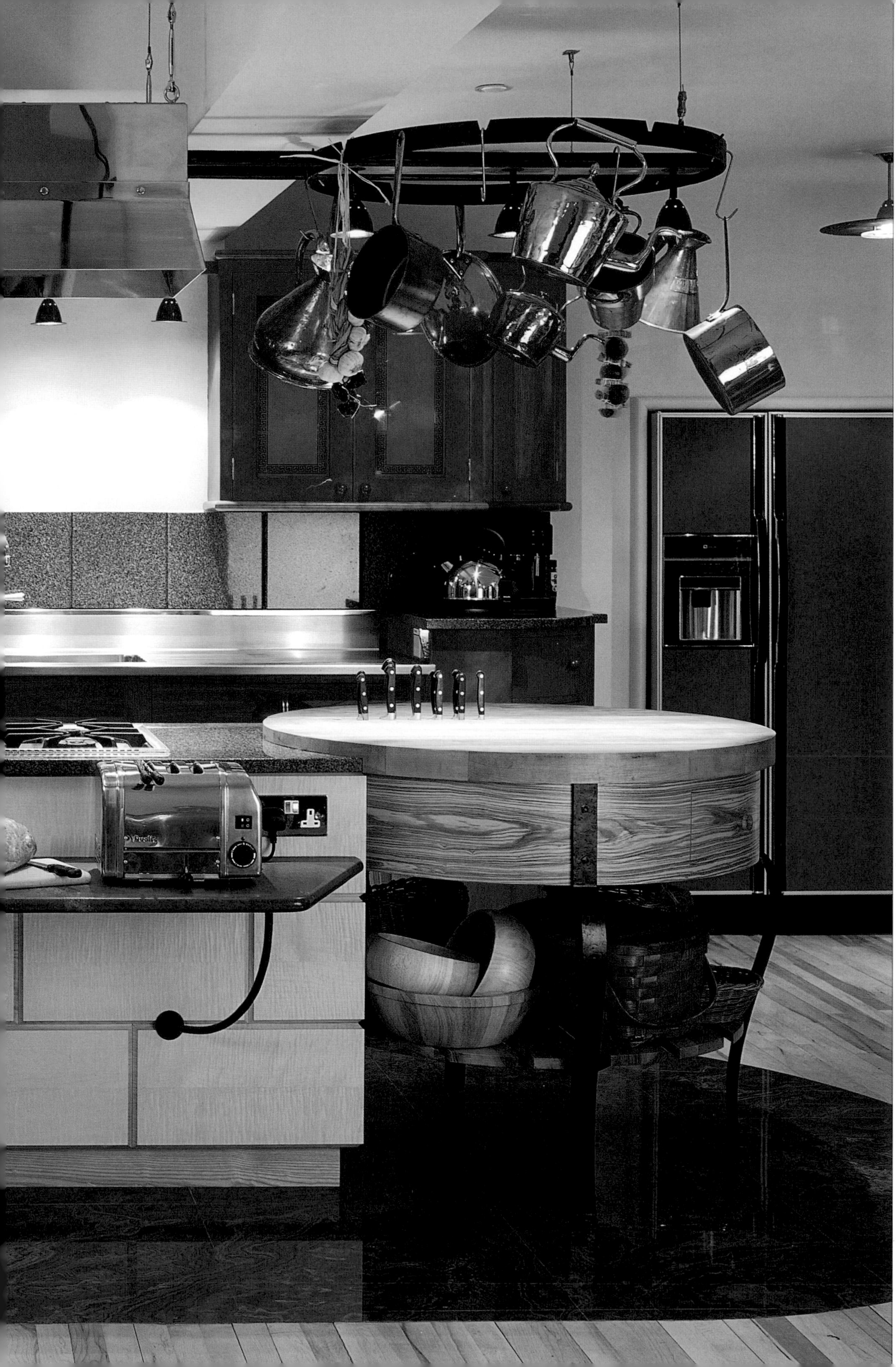

ROOM PLANS

SMALL KITCHEN PLAN

IN A SMALL ROOM, focus on your primary kitchen needs, mapping out the area for the stove, the sink, and food preparation. Establish the minimum dimensions you can work within without feeling cramped, and then arrange other appliances and storage around this core. Capitalize on every available space from floor to ceiling, and select durable finishes that can adapt to a variety of uses.

TALL APPLIANCE STACK
Solid floor-to-ceiling units are placed around a corner to minimize their impact.

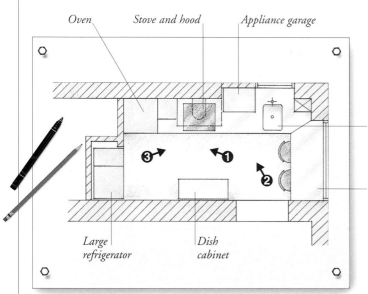

Oven   Stove and hood   Appliance garage

INTERNAL ROOM DIMENSIONS:
6ft 2in (1.9m) WIDE
14ft 4in (4.4m) LONG

Single sink

Eating bar

Large refrigerator   Dish cabinet

△ BIRD'S-EYE VIEW
The sink and eating areas benefit from the best natural light and window views, and the stovetop is against an outside wall to ensure good ventilation. Other kitchen appliances sit behind cabinetry so as not to obstruct the flow of traffic.

REFRIGERATOR
A large refrigerator is concealed behind cabinetry to make it less obtrusive.

PANTRY CABINET
A pull-out pantry sits next to the refrigerator; different foods can be picked up in one trip.

DESIGN POINTS

■ In a small space, the close proximity of tasks is inevitable, but check that you can move about the room freely.

■ Install eye-level appliances in tall cabinets at one end of the room and try to leave the rest open to create a feeling of space in a small room.

■ Check that counters can double up for other activities. In this kitchen, the eating bar is also used for food preparation.

■ Some appliances have reverse hinging – doors opening in the opposite direction may solve a few of your space problems.

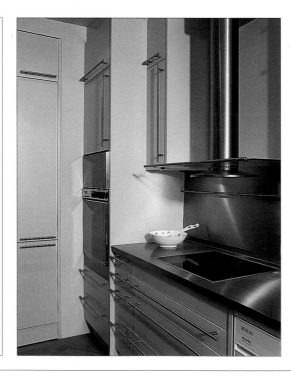

STORAGE CABINET
Storage facilities are designed to fit in above and below major appliances.

EYE-LEVEL OVEN
Hot dishes from the tall oven unit can be set down quickly on the counter to the right.

GLASS-FRONTED UNIT
Dishes and glassware are displayed within reach of the dishwasher.

◁ ❶ OPENING UP THE SPACE
The halogen stovetop sits flush against the counter, and can serve as a preparation area when not in use. A single cabinet, a slender hood, and task lights keep this area bright and open.

HOOD
A slimline hood removes food odors and steam, which can be a problem in small kitchens.

❷ **DURABLE FINISHES** ▷
Stainless steel is used on every horizontal surface because it is heat- and water-resistant, while the cabinets below have a tough melamine finish to protect them from knocks in a tight workplace.

APPLIANCE "GARAGE"
This utilizes the full depth of the counter; an appliance can be stored at the back and pulled out onto the worksurface when needed.

WINDOW VIEW
The sink has a view to make washing dishes a more enjoyable task.

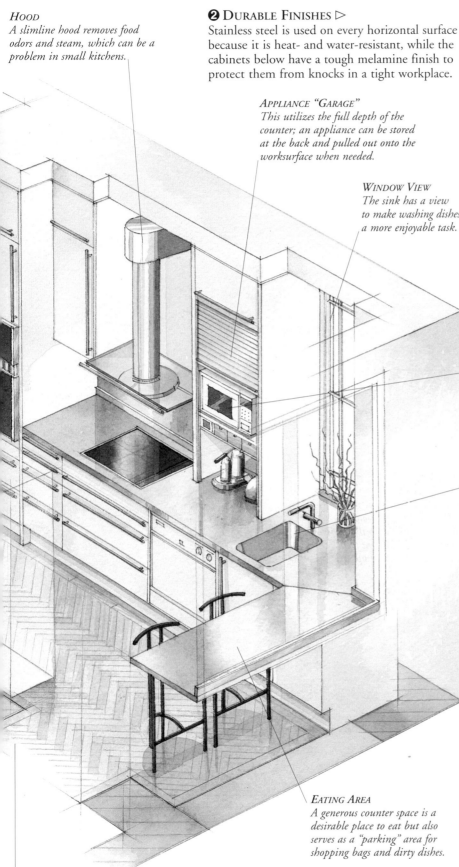

EYE-LEVEL MICROWAVE
The oven is placed at an accessible height, leaving the countertop free.

SINGLE SINK
A small sink saves on precious counter space. Use it for washing food and rinsing dishes before placing them in the dishwasher below.

> ### FOR MORE DETAILS...
>
> *Appliance "garage"* SEE P24
>
> *Halogen stovetop* SEE P28
>
> *Eye-level double oven* SEE P31
>
> *Eating bar* SEE P32
>
> *Stainless-steel counters* SEE P38

EATING AREA
A generous counter space is a desirable place to eat but also serves as a "parking" area for shopping bags and dirty dishes.

WOOD FLOORING
A natural beech floor adds warmth and offsets the hard, industrial finishes used elsewhere.

❸ **NATURAL LIGHT** ▷
The light-reflective qualities of stainless steel, together with an open undercounter space and tall windows, make this end of the kitchen feel both light and airy.

SMALL KITCHEN CHOICE

△ MAXIMIZING FLOOR SPACE
A handmade kitchen can be an efficient choice, as furniture can be tailor-made to fit the space. Here, the appliances sit in a tall stack, while the area beneath the stovetop is kept free to make the kitchen feel spacious.

FORM FOLLOWS FUNCTION ▷
A straight run of cabinets is arranged in a logical sequence, with the sink between the stove and food preparation area. Above and below counter level, well-designed cabinets offer distinct open and closed storage areas.

◁ KITCHENS WITHOUT WINDOWS
Every available space from floor to ceiling has been filled in this tiny kitchen without windows. Strong task lighting, a simple palette of materials, cool colors, and open shelving produce a calm, orderly result.

MOVING IN CIRCLES ▷
A circular kitchen fits comfortably into a room 9ft 6in (2.9m) wide. The centralized arrangement of activities, with the cook in the middle, makes movement between different work stations highly efficient.

UNFITTED KITCHEN PLAN

UNLIKE "FITTED" KITCHENS, in which standard cabinets run from wall to wall, the "unfitted" kitchen takes a less formal approach. It is home to a collection of hand-crafted pieces that stand alone, and although the sink cabinet is still built-in, the overall effect is of individual elements with separate tasks, working together to create a smooth-running whole.

△ ❶ CLOSE PROXIMITY
The cooking and preparation zones occupy their own distinct areas within the kitchen but sit only two steps away from each other, for maximum efficiency.

DESIGN POINTS

■ Imagine activity and storage areas as separate pieces of free-standing furniture. Buy items from a variety of sources and enjoy the differences of shape, height, color, and finish that each one has to offer.

■ Retain or uncover existing architectural features, such as fireplaces and alcoves, to add character to the room.

■ Where possible, allow space around each piece of furniture, but make sure all the essential facilities are conveniently close to one another. Try to keep the cooking and food preparation areas as the focus of the room.

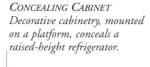

CONCEALING CABINET
Decorative cabinetry, mounted on a platform, conceals a raised-height refrigerator.

AGA
Self-contained in its own tiled alcove, this five-door Aga stove is the main cooking center.

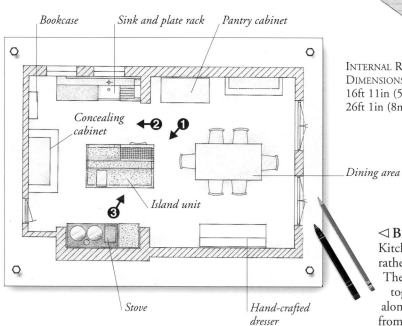

Bookcase   Sink and plate rack   Pantry cabinet

Concealing cabinet

Island unit

Stove   *Hand-crafted dresser*

INTERNAL ROOM DIMENSIONS:
16ft 11in (5.2m) WIDE
26ft 1in (8m) LONG

DRESSER
Occupying one wall of the dining area, a dresser provides open-shelf storage with doors and drawers below.

Dining area

◁ BIRD'S-EYE VIEW
Kitchen furniture fills the room, rather than sitting at the edges. The elements are not linked together by counters but stand alone, and can be approached from more than one direction.

BOOKCASE
A wall-mounted bookcase, with a wine rack below, utilizes the corner space without making the room feel overcrowded.

❷ CONTRASTING ELEMENTS ▷
Standing side by side, the difference in height, style, and finish between the concealing cabinet and the bookcase emphasizes the separate functions of these pieces of furniture, while enhancing the furnished feel of the room.

CENTRAL ISLAND
The chopping and food preparation area is divided up into granite and butcher block surfaces at different heights.

PANTRY
Space in front of the cabinet ensures that the wide doors can be left open when restocking.

FOR MORE DETAILS...

Pantry cabinet SEE PP18–19

Refrigerator SEE PP20–21

Aga stove SEE P30

Rectangular table SEE P33

Tiles SEE PP42–43

PARLOR CUPBOARD
Wall-mounted to free the floor space around the eating area, this custom-made cabinet stores china, table linen, and breakfast cereals.

FRENCH WINDOWS
Next to the eating area, large windows provide natural light and a view of the outdoors.

REFECTORY TABLE
Generous space around the table allows up to 10 people to enjoy a meal in comfort.

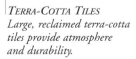

TERRA-COTTA TILES
Large, reclaimed terra-cotta tiles provide atmosphere and durability.

❸ STORAGE FACILITIES ▷
A tall pantry cabinet rather than a row of base and wall cabinets is an efficient use of space. Everyday dishes sit on a wall-mounted plate rack, and baskets hang on hooks from a soffit.

UNFITTED KITCHEN CHOICE

△ SIMPLE STAND-ALONE FURNITURE
The simplicity of freestanding kitchen furniture is very appealing, and here the combination of painted wood and white walls adds to the effect. The space around each item is important, so avoid continuous runs of units, to prevent cluttering up every wall and corner.

△ ROOM DIVIDERS
In an unfitted kitchen, there is more scope to use old pieces of furniture. The antique pine dresser in the foreground acts as a room divider, separating off the cooking and eating areas. New cabinets provide counter space and storage close to the stove.

RETAINING ORIGINAL FEATURES ▷
A well-furnished kitchen can combine both freestanding and built-in items successfully. Here, a sitting room was converted to make a large kitchen. Some features were kept intact, such as the ceiling moldings and the chimney; the stovetop and oven sit inside the alcove and use the flue for ventilation.

△ APPLIANCES BEHIND DOORS
A well-proportioned cabinet can be an attractive and convenient home for large appliances. In this kitchen, a refrigerator and microwave are built into the cabinet but it could just as easily contain an eye-level oven and a pantry for fresh and nonperishable foods.

△ ACCESSIBLE STORAGE
The most useful storage space is between knee height and eye level; in a large cabinet the space offered at this level is greater than in a series of cabinets above and below the counter. Above all, a tall storage unit is a feature and a relief from the uniformity of similar-height cabinets.

BUILT-IN KITCHEN PLAN

IMAGINATION AND resourcefulness are needed to design a kitchen using standard built-in cabinets. The secret is to be selective, so that your kitchen is not overwhelmed by repetitive cabinetry. Pick doors, drawers, and glass-fronted units from a standard line, and then shop around for counters, flooring, and lighting to reflect personal taste.

WALL COVERING
A cream, oil-based paint lightens the room and is easy to wipe clean.

BLACKBOARD
A leftover cabinet door has been coated in blackboard paint to create a message board.

△ ❶ UTILITY CLOSET
A tall two-door unit, designed to hold a refrigerator, has been adapted to create a large storage cabinet for essential cleaning equipment.

HALF-DEPTH WALL UNIT
A gap between the unit and the counter leaves space for electrical wall sockets.

DESIGN POINTS

■ Try to create visual interest by avoiding very long runs of similar cabinets with the same door fronts. Break up the monotony by leaving wall space for shelves and pictures.

■ Consider how to balance the horizontal and vertical lines in a built-in kitchen. Blocks of tall cabinets, adjacent to the wall, can remove the tyranny of long counters and wall units.

■ To make a built-in kitchen less clinical, try customizing units. Hire a carpenter to build a dresser above base units or, as a cheaper alternative, adapt existing carcasses and paint the insides in bright colors.

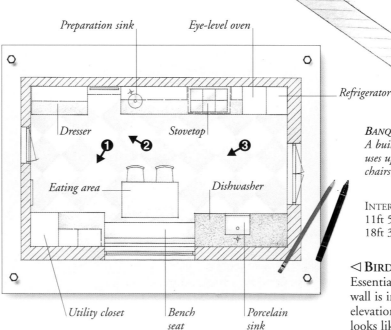

Preparation sink
Eye-level oven
Refrigerator
Dresser
Stovetop
Eating area
Dishwasher
Utility closet
Bench seat
Porcelain sink

BANQUETTE
A built-in window seat uses up less space than four chairs around a table.

INTERNAL ROOM DIMENSIONS:
11ft 5in (3.5m) WIDE
18ft 3in (5.6m) LONG

◁ BIRD'S-EYE VIEW
Essentially a narrow room, each long wall is intensively used, but clever elevations underlie what in the plan looks like a plain row of cabinets.

CUSTOM-MADE DRESSER
The top of the dresser is edged with leftover wood molding, for decoration.

TOWEL RACK
A hanging rack is a useful device to fill a wall left intentionally free of cabinets.

VEGETABLE SINK
Fresh ingredients can be rinsed at the preparation site, preventing a journey across the kitchen.

FOR MORE DETAILS...

Vegetable sink SEE P26

Lacquered wood counters SEE P39

Linoleum floor SEE P45

Ceiling can lights SEE P46

HOOD AND STOVETOP
The choice of a stylish aluminum hood and five- rather than four-ring burner stovetop helps personalize this kitchen.

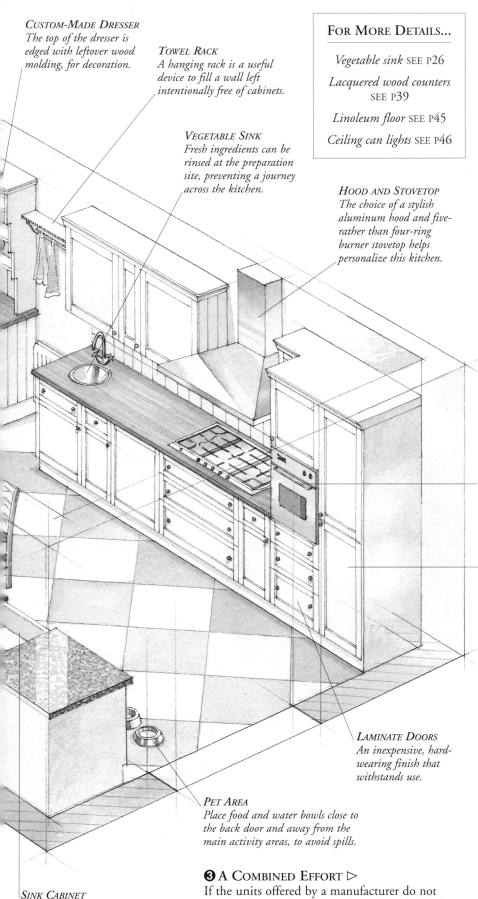

△ ❷ **ATTENTION TO DETAIL**
Simple additions can make all the difference. Here, a dresser has been built above a standard cabinet, and thin beech counters are edged with 1½ in (40mm) strips to make them look more solid.

EYE-LEVEL OVEN
Place a storage cabinet above and drawers below to vary the appearance of the cabinets.

REFRIGERATOR HOUSING
The oven and refrigerator sit next to each other and must be well insulated to save energy.

LAMINATE DOORS
An inexpensive, hard-wearing finish that withstands use.

PET AREA
Place food and water bowls close to the back door and away from the main activity areas, to avoid spills.

❸ **A COMBINED EFFORT** ▷
If the units offered by a manufacturer do not match your needs, commission a handmade piece of kitchen furniture to your specifications, as in the case of this space-saving window seat.

SINK CABINET
The sink is fitted into a standard cabinet, but durable granite countertops add individuality.

BUILT-IN KITCHEN CHOICE

△ BOLD PLANNING

The design of this kitchen brings the built-in cabinets into the center of the room rather than placing them around the walls. The stove and sink face each other so that the cook can enjoy two different views when working. Painted plaster walls offset cool stainless steel.

△ STANDARD CABINETS

A low-budget kitchen uses a standard row of base units to create maximum counter and storage space. The large preparation area has been adapted to suit the cook's needs by adding a small sink for rinsing fresh foods.

QUALITY AND COMFORT ▷

Made to last, this kitchen is manufactured using durable materials, such as ceramic floor tiles, granite, and stainless steel. It combines high-tech materials with traditional wood finishes, to add the warmth and comfort associated with English country kitchens.

△ BEHIND CLOSED DOORS

The choice of all-white matching finishes on the cabinetry and walls helps brighten this narrow kitchen, which is annexed off a larger room. Eye-level, wall-mounted cabinets have been abandoned in favor of floor-to-ceiling cabinets along the entrance corridor.

△ COLOR VARIATION

The cabinets have been chosen from a standard line so that they fit imaginatively into the room plan. A run of base cabinets surrounds the eating area and doubles as a serving counter. Their bright painted blue finish adds character to the room, which can be difficult to achieve in built-in kitchens.

ISLAND KITCHEN PLAN

A CENTRAL ISLAND is the key to a large, sociable kitchen because the cook is able to look into the room rather than at a blank wall. In spatial terms, an island arrangement helps concentrate cooking activities into a small zone so that the cook does not have to waste time traveling backward and forward across the entire room.

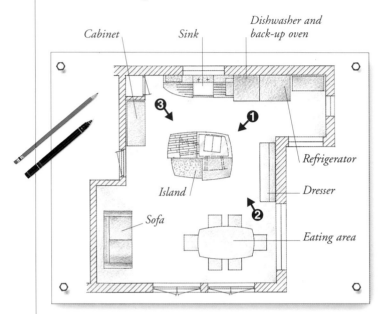

Cabinet   *Sink*   *Dishwasher and back-up oven*

Refrigerator

Dresser

Island

Sofa

Eating area

INTERNAL ROOM DIMENSIONS:
15ft 4in (4.7m) WIDE
20ft 10in (6.4m) LONG

PLATE RACK
A wall-mounted rack drip-dries and stores wet plates direct from the dishwasher or adjacent sink.

LARGE SINK
A deep sink is suitable for soaking oven pans, while heavy pots need only be carried a short distance from the stovetop for draining.

△ BIRD'S-EYE VIEW
For an island to be successful, it needs space around it. Allow 3ft 10in (1.2m) between the island and the wall cabinets. If a sink is directly behind the work area, ensure there is at least 3ft 3in (1m) so that two people can work back to back.

DESIGN POINTS

■ Allow space between key activities on the island – the wooden cutting board and gas stove should be 18in (45cm) apart to prevent heat damage and fire risk.

■ Plan a low-level counter for operating electrical appliances on the island. If finished in cold marble or granite, it can double as a pastry area.

■ Lighting is important in a kitchen used for both cooking and entertaining. Ensure that the island is well lit from above so that you are not working in shadow, and install lights on dimmer switches to create soft ambient lighting in eating and relaxation areas.

CUTTING BOARD
Positioned with a view of the table and garden beyond, the cutting board is close to the sink, stovetop, and refrigerator.

STORAGE CABINET
Bulky hardware is stored just behind the island.

LOW-LEVEL COUNTER
Built-in electrical sockets make it possible to use food processors and other electrical appliances on the island.

◁ ❶ SOCIABLE COOKING
The gas stovetop and undercounter oven face toward the blue sofa so that the cook can talk to guests. A stainless-steel turn-up at the back protects the lacquered serving counter from oil and spills.

DISHWASHER STACK
An eye-level oven rests on top of a raised dishwasher to reduce the need to bend.

❷ EYE-CATCHING CABINETRY ▷
The serving-counter cabinet is the most decorative of the island zones, as it is seen from the table. It hides the stove, making it easier to cook in front of an audience without inhibition.

REFRIGERATOR
The island plan frees up space around the walls for a refrigerator a short distance from the preparation area.

STAINLESS-STEEL STOVETOP
The counters that flank the stovetop are heatproof. Allow at least 12in (30cm) on either side.

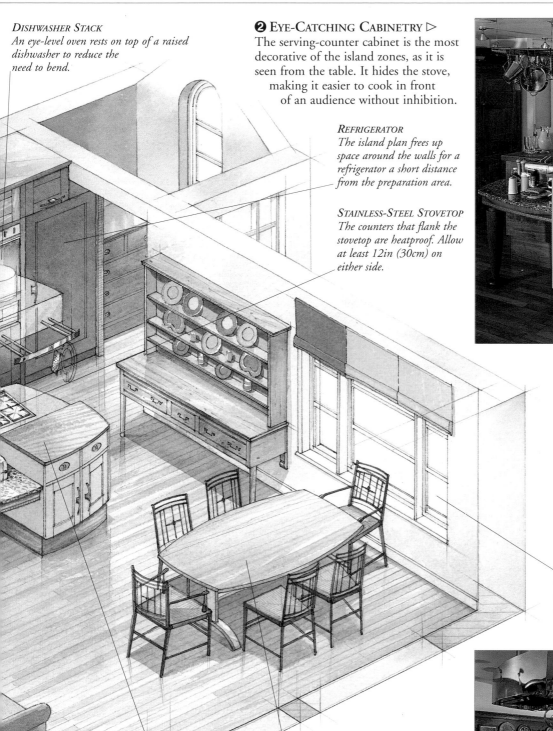

FOR MORE DETAILS...

Center island unit
SEE PP24–25

Stovetops and hoods
SEE PP28–29

Storage cabinet SEE P36

Lighting SEE PP46–47

WINDOWS
A wall of windows, plus glass doors leading to the yard, fill the room with light.

KITCHEN TABLE
Placed in the brightest corner of the kitchen, the family table has an oiled wood surface to make it hard-wearing.

SERVING AREA
A free counter for serving food, between the cooking zone and the table, makes entertaining easy.

RELAXATION AREA
Space for a sitting area is made possible by focusing appliances and counters in the center of the kitchen.

❸ FULL PARTICIPATION ▷
Trips back to the stove mid-meal to perform the finishing touches to a dish are no longer a chore, as the cook is not excluded from round-table talks.

ISLAND KITCHEN CHOICE

△ MULTIFUNCTIONAL PENINSULA UNIT

In a small kitchen, where counter space is limited and there is no room for a table, consider a circular half butcher block and half granite peninsula unit. The custom-made area will easily double as a food preparation and eating area without taking up valuable floor space.

△ MINIMALIST ISLAND

A brushed stainless-steel island unit with a small, molded sink gives the extroverted cook the facilities to wash and prepare fresh ingredients while entertaining guests, who can perch on stools at the other side.

VARIABLE-HEIGHT ISLAND ▷

A central island works best if it has been divided into four key activity zones, each arranged at the most efficient height to perform the required tasks. Unlike most built-in kitchens, where runs of counters are arranged around the kitchen walls, the island enables you to occupy center stage.

△ CENTRAL SINK AREA

If your kitchen has no spectacular window view, build the sink into an island so that you can face the room rather than a blank wall when performing this mundane task. Here, the sink is thoughtfully placed so that you simply turn around to use the stove.

△ SLENDER ISLAND WORKING TABLE WITH RAISED-HEIGHT PLATFORM

A narrow kitchen can accommodate a long modern or traditional working table that acts as a central workspace for several people at once. A removable preparation platform at one end of the table allows you to stand and prepare meals while supervising children's activities.

IMPROVISED KITCHEN PLAN

ONCE YOU UNDERSTAND the principles of ergonomic kitchen design, it is possible to assemble a comfortable and easy-to-use kitchen on a tight budget. The secret is to improvise, so rather than just settling for low-cost cabinets, scour junk shops and auctions for furniture that can be adapted for kitchen use, and bring inherited items, which you may have placed elsewhere, into the kitchen.

APOTHECARY DRAWERS
Drawers picked up at auction store spices, candles, and other household items.

PORCELAIN SINK
Inherited intact, this porcelain sink with a drainboard is built into a homemade kitchen cabinet.

△ **❶ CONTAINED SPACE**
As space is limited, the sink, stove, and preparation area butt up against one another, but this compact arrangement works well.

DESIGN POINTS

■ Thoughtful selection of items is necessary; make sure that they are functional, and measure each piece of furniture to check that there is room.

■ The most problematic area is around the sink. Think about the amount of drainboard space – allow 24in (60cm) on one side. Consider how the counter joins the basin – it needs a high-performance seal. Also, the area behind the sink needs protection from water splashes (*see pp42–43*).

■ Finding furniture with good work surfaces may be difficult. Assess your priorities to see whether you can install new counters (*see pp38–39*).

INTERNAL ROOM DIMENSIONS:
6ft 2in (1.9m) WIDE
15ft 4in (4.7m) LONG

Spice drawers

HARDWARE STORAGE
A china cabinet and cutlery drawer below the sink allow items to be put away as soon as they have been washed.

WOODEN BENCH
With no room for a table, a bench provides a place for guests to sit.

Stove   *Food preparation area*

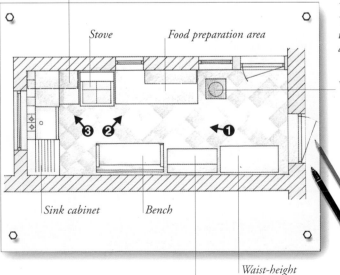

Wood-burning stove

Sink cabinet   *Bench*

◁ **BIRD'S-EYE VIEW**
The sink, stove, and a long food preparation counter form an L-shape of built-in cabinetry, while unfitted cabinets and a bench sit up close, leaving space for the sink cabinet doors to open.

Small cabinet

Waist-height storage cabinet

FREESTANDING GAS STOVE
This upright gas appliance has a fold-away grill at eye level. Easy-to-watch, eye-level grills are only found on old stoves.

REFRIGERATOR
Installed undercounter directly below the food preparation area, a small refrigerator squeezes into a narrow space, and is inexpensive.

FOR MORE DETAILS...

Undercounter refrigerator SEE P20

Oven cooking SEE P30

Sink cabinet SEE P34

Wall coverings SEE PP42–43

STORAGE SHELF
An old pine shelf provides open storage above the counter for utensils and equipment, and keeps the countertop free.

△ ❷ **PROTECTIVE MEASURES**
In this narrow kitchen, the wood counter abuts the stove. To keep the wood surface intact, hot pans from the stove are always put down on trivets.

VIEW
Clever planning means that the work surface sits between two windows and is flooded with natural light.

WOOD-BURNING STOVE
A cast-iron stove provides extra "parking" space for items close to the food preparation counter.

TERRA-COTTA TILES
Tiles, bought from an old farmhouse and cleaned, make durable flooring.

❸ **LOW-COST MATERIALS** ▷
Painted wood boards are employed to great effect to cover up an uneven ceiling. It is also used to build low-cost cabinetry below the sink and the wood counters.

PANTRY CABINET
A waist-height unit makes an improvised pantry cabinet.

IMPROVISED KITCHEN CHOICE

△ AFFORDABLE STAINLESS STEEL

If you like the qualities of stainless steel but cannot afford it, try a catering auction where secondhand professional kitchen equipment is sold at a good price. Try to buy a stainless-steel workbench and a sink to provide a basic dishwashing, preparation, and bar eating area.

△ EQUIPMENT RACKS

Utensils hanging on the wall not only look attractive but are stored within easy reach of the counter. Here, three stainless-steel towel racks have been installed to make a hanging device. For a longer counter, try using a bar taken from an old armoire.

WALL DISPLAY ▷

In small, narrow kitchens, there is often not the room for a desk in which to store meal plans or lists of household tasks. Instead, put up a bulletin board and attach favourite recipes, food lists, and bills for safe keeping.

△ INEXPENSIVE FACELIFT

If it is not within your budget to change the design of your kitchen to suit your specific needs, transform its appearance by painting the cabinets in a strong color and changing the door handles. On a bigger budget, new counters and lighting make a huge difference.

△ DO-IT-YOURSELF SHELVING

Open shelves with hooks are relatively easy to construct and have the capacity to store a variety of kitchen equipment above counter level. Although a less expensive alternative to custom-made cabinets, items stored in this way will gather dust and need to be brought down regularly for cleaning.

FAMILY KITCHEN CHOICE

△ CHILDREN'S COOKING SHELF
The low slate shelf that runs along the front edge of the island provides an indestructible child-height counter for younger members of the family who enjoy cooking. At other times, it functions as a preparation center for operating electrical appliances, and a breakfast bar.

△ EATING TOGETHER
The kitchen table is the focal point of family life, so even when space is limited, try to include a table in your plan. A small, round table, about 4ft (1.2m) in diameter seats four. When not in use, the chairs can be tucked in closer to the table.

CREATIVE ACTIVITIES ▷
A family kitchen table is not only used at mealtimes but for a variety of activities, such as painting, drawing, and model-making. Choose an old pine table where blemishes will not be too obvious, or cover the table with a waterproof tablecloth for protection.

△ TOY DRAWER
Toys scattered all over the floor are likely to cause accidents, so plan a pull-out drawer where toys can be quickly stowed away as mealtime approaches. An easy-to-clean floor covering, such as sheet vinyl, is advisable.

△ KITCHEN OFFICE
A desk area in the kitchen can be useful for organizing both household administration and helping children with their homework while you are involved in kitchen tasks. A bulletin board and blackboard for notes and shopping lists also help your household run smoothly.

PLAN YOUR DESIGN

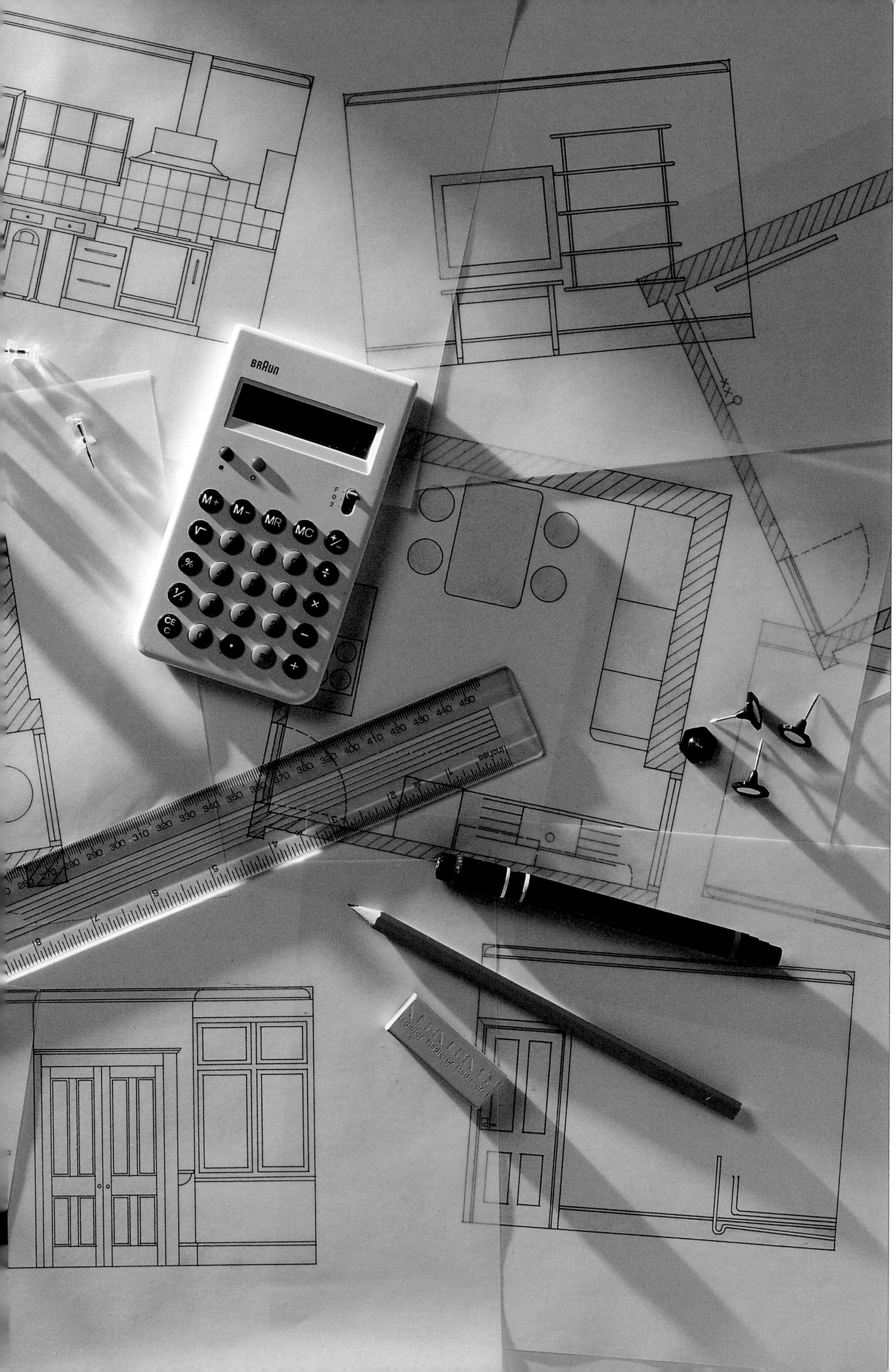

PLAN YOUR ROOM

THE FLOOR PLAN and elevations are the starting point for any new kitchen design. Use the following simple step-by-step guide to help you map out a survey of the room, and then to transfer your measurements onto graph paper to create accurate scale drawings.

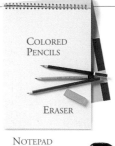

COLORED PENCILS

ERASER

NOTEPAD

EQUIPMENT
To help you create an accurate visual record of the room's dimensions, plumbing and electrical outlets, and architectural features, you will need this basic equipment.

CAMERA

TAPE MEASURE

STEPLADDER

FLOOR DIMENSIONS

Before you begin work on a new kitchen design, you must familiarize yourself with the features of the room that you have chosen as your kitchen. Accurate measurements of the floor area will help you work out whether an appliance or piece of furniture will fit comfortably into the available space. A survey of electrical outlets, natural light sources, outside walls, and kitchen access will help you plan the best location for food preparation, cooking, eating, and clean-up areas in your new kitchen.

❶ SKETCH THE ROOM
Stand in the middle of the room and look down at the floor. Hand-draw a rough sketch of the floor area in a notepad with a soft pencil. Draw in the shapes of fixed furniture or architectural features to be incorporated into your new design.

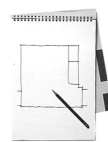

❷ PLOT THE DIMENSIONS
Next, measure the total floor area. Place the tape measure across the room, and jot down the length on your sketch in colored pencil or pen. At this stage, it is simpler to ignore surface details, such as baseboards, in your calculations.

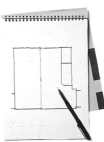

❸ PLOT THE WALLS
Following the room around in a clockwise direction, so that you don't get confused, measure each wall length in turn. Do not assume that the walls are symmetrical, and carefully mark down the measurements on your sketch for future reference.

❹ PLOT OUTLETS
Survey the room for outlets, such as gas and water supply and electrical sockets. If present, plot their position on your survey. Indicate structural features to be incorporated into the design – chimney flues, outside walls, and room orientation.

❺ PLOT FIXED FEATURES
Measure the dimensions and position in the room of any appliances or cabinetry you do not wish to move, such as a stove or a pantry, and then draw them onto your sketch. Remember, though, most kitchen items are fairly inexpensive to relocate.

❻ PHOTOGRAPH ODD CORNERS
Take photographs to help you record areas where it is hard to measure the dimensions, perhaps in awkward corners or on sloping walls. Photographs of features in the room, such as fireplaces, will also help you recall style details when designing a new kitchen.

WALL ELEVATIONS

Although you do not need very detailed elevations to design your new kitchen, it is useful to have a sketch survey of each of the four walls. These sketches help establish whether there is enough wall space for freestanding furniture without blocking windows, radiators, or other fixed features. With elevations, you can also visualize what size furniture would best suit the proportions of the room.

❶ MEASURE THE HEIGHT
Stand facing one wall and draw a rough sketch of it. Draw in doors, windows, or alcoves. Architectural details, like wall moldings, are not yet important. Stand on a stepladder and measure the wall height from floor to ceiling. Note it on the sketch.

❷ MEASURE THE DOORS
Record the height and width of any doors, baseboards, and cornices, plus the details of any surrounding frames or decorative moldings. Note the dimensions of the outlets that you may not wish to obstruct. Draw an elevation sketch for each wall.

DRAWING UP SCALE PLANS

The rough sketch survey of the existing room plan (*see p76*) contains all the information you need to work out where appliances and furniture can be placed within your new kitchen. However, if you wish to take the design further, you may want to draw up the plan and elevations to scale. Follow the instructions below.

GRAPH PAPER

PEN

T-SQUARE

LONG RULER

OUTSIDE WALLS
A thick border of cross-hatching indicates outside walls.

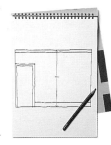

YOU WILL NEED
Imperial and metric graph paper is supplied with this book, but you will also need the equipment shown above.

◁ **❶ TRANSFER THE FLOOR PLAN**
Refer to your rough plan for precise measurements, and then accurately plot the four perimeter walls to scale on graph paper. Join up straight lines with a T-square. Next, plot key features such as outside walls, doors, and windows that are important for planning your new kitchen.

DOOR HINGING
A dotted line indicates the direction in which the door swings open.

❷ DRAW UP AN ELEVATION ▷
Referring to the measurements on your sketch elevations, draw up each wall to scale. Work from the floor upward, marking on details and outlets last.

DOORKNOB
Indicate the way the door opens by drawing on the door handle.

❸ OTHER ELEVATIONS ▽
Draw each of the remaining elevations to scale, marking on relevant details to give you a complete picture of the room before you begin the design.

LIGHT
Parallel lines show a window as a light source.

CORNICE HEIGHT
The width of the cornice will limit the height of tall cabinetry.

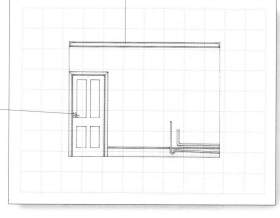

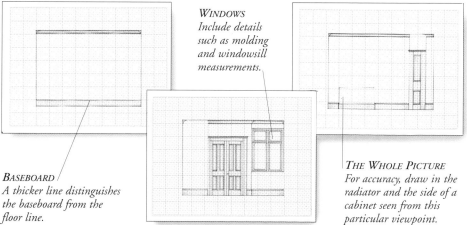

BASEBOARD
A thicker line distinguishes the baseboard from the floor line.

WINDOWS
Include details such as molding and windowsill measurements.

THE WHOLE PICTURE
For accuracy, draw in the radiator and the side of a cabinet seen from this particular viewpoint.

PLACE THE FEATURES

REFER TO THE LIST you have compiled of your chosen kitchen appliances, furniture, and materials, and you should have all the information you need to plan a kitchen that suits your personality and needs. The next step is to find a successful way of arranging the features in your designated space. Try out several different arrangements by placing a piece of tracing paper over the scaled-up room plan (*see pp76–77*), and drawing on the elements, following the order of design (*see right*). You may draw several versions before reaching the best solution.

TRACING PAPER

MASKING TAPE

T-SQUARE

YOU WILL NEED ▷
Take the room plan that you have drawn to scale, and stick a sheet of tracing paper over the top with masking tape. Place the features using a soft pencil, long ruler, and T-square. When you want to explore a new design, start fresh on a clean sheet of tracing paper.

PEN
PENCIL
ERASER

LONG
RULER

ORDER OF DESIGN

When designing your new kitchen layout, place your chosen elements on the room plan in the following order, to avoid confusion.

❶ **PLACE THE SINK CABINET** first on your plan because, including drainboards, it is the longest unit. Arrange the cooking area, preparation area, and dishwasher close by.

❷ **POSITION THE STOVE** a few steps from the sink so that you can deal with pots and pans without having to walk across the kitchen. Consider where to place an oven.

❸ **PLAN THE PREPARATION AREA** within reach of the stove but also a short distance from the sink for rinsing fresh ingredients.

❹ **PLACE THE REFRIGERATOR** away from the main traffic area around the sink, but close to the preparation zone and kitchen table.

❺ **POSITION THE TABLE** near a natural light source and away from activity areas. Plan wall-mounted and undercounter storage facilities within reach of activity centers.

REJECTED PLANS

Arriving at a well-planned, ergonomic design takes time, especially if the room contains fixed features that have to be incorporated into the design. Let your kitchen plan evolve, and learn from the designs that you reject in the process.

RESTRICTED ACCESS ▽
A double sink and dining area are planned, but both are crowded. The sink faces the wall and is overhung by wall units, while the table and refrigerator restrict access to the room.

REDUCED STORAGE ▽
The counter is increased by a peninsula, but the refrigerator is now across the room. The table is under the window but the cabinet has been halved in size to make more space.

WALL CABINETS
Eye-level cabinets over the sink make this corner cramped.

EATING AREA
The table seats only three and projects into the room, blocking the entrance.

SINK AREA
The corner space is crowded, but the food preparation area is greater.

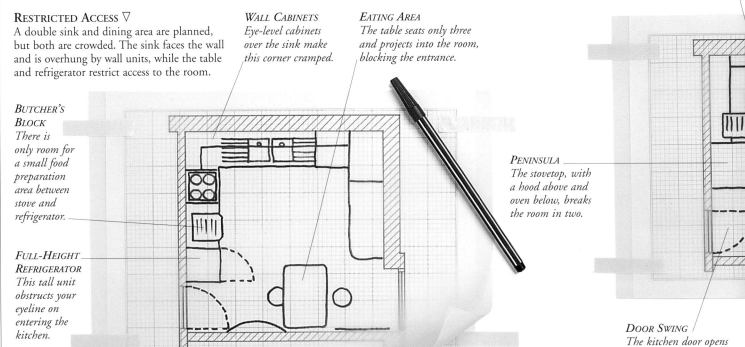

BUTCHER'S BLOCK
There is only room for a small food preparation area between stove and refrigerator.

FULL-HEIGHT REFRIGERATOR
This tall unit obstructs your eyeline on entering the kitchen.

PENINSULA
The stovetop, with a hood above and oven below, breaks the room in two.

DOOR SWING
The kitchen door opens onto the peninsula, crowding entry.

SUCCESSFUL PLAN

Having resolved how best to arrange the appliances within the space, and if satisfied that you have found an ergonomic solution, plot your final design onto graph paper in ink.

NEW WINDOW
This is installed in an outside wall to create access to natural light for the double sink.

RAISED-HEIGHT DISHWASHER
Placed between the sink and a built-in cabinet, dishes are rinsed before washing and then put away afterward.

BOILER CABINET
The boiler cannot be moved, and so this corner unit has to be fitted into the design.

STOVE AND UNDERCOUNTER OVEN
These appliances are surrounded by a heat-resistant granite counter and are within reach of the sink.

BUILT-IN CABINET
An original cabinet is left intact, and is adapted to house both a refrigerator and china storage.

PREPARATION AREA
A circular half end-grain and half granite block provides a large counter close to the stove without breaking up the space.

TELEPHONE SHELF
A narrow ledge added onto the cabinet is a useful space for a telephone, within reach of the table.

DOOR OPENING
Rehung so that it opens against the right-hand wall, it allows an open view of the kitchen. Also, more than one person can prepare food at the circle without having to close the door first.

WINDOW
The original window lights this end of the room.

WALL SHELVES
A narrow set of curved shelves fit on the wall between the door and table without taking up valuable floor space.

SMALL TABLE
Pushed against the wall close to the window to save space, it can be pulled out to seat four.

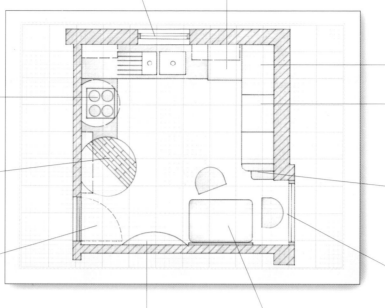

STORAGE
A cabinet above the dishwasher, a plate rack, and shelves provide minimum storage.

LIMITED COUNTER SPACE ▽
The sink cabinet fits next to the window but trips from the sink to the stove are interrupted by people entering and leaving the room. Floor-to-ceiling storage units take priority over counters, which take up only a small area by the stove.

EATING AREA
Poorly placed at the dark end of the room, the table is surrounded by tall cabinets.

CENTRAL SPACE
There is too much unused space in the center, because of poor planning.

FULL-HEIGHT REFRIGERATOR
This is housed in the remaining half of the built-in cabinet.

COUNTER
There is only space for a small counter next to the stove for food preparation.

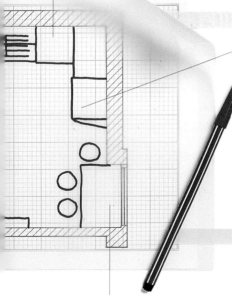

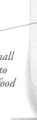

TABLE IN WINDOW
A fixed table is inflexible, and part of the built-in cabinet has been removed to make room for seats.

ENTRANCE DOOR
Kitchen traffic can interrupt the flow between sink and stove.

APPLIANCE STACK
An oven and dishwasher stack near the door crowds the entrance.

PLANNING DETAIL

WHEN YOU HAVE arrived at a satisfactory floor plan, you can start to consider the finer details. Choose cabinet finishes, wall coverings, flooring, and lighting that match your kitchen needs, but keep in mind your budget and the amount of time you have allowed for the work.

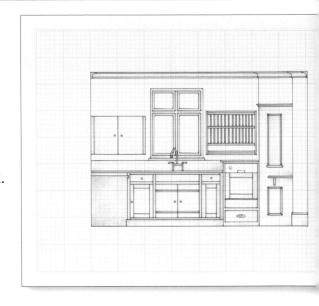

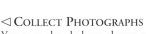

◁ COLLECT PHOTOGRAPHS
You may already have chosen specific appliances and cabinets to fit limited floor space; if not, pictures from magazines and catalogs will help you clarify the style you want, whether traditional, modern, or high-tech.

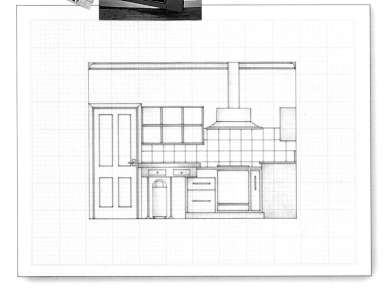

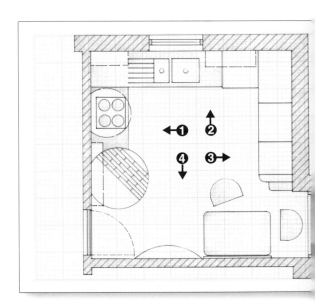

△ ❶ COOKING AND PREPARATION ZONE
Draw in wall-mounted and undercounter cabinets to see in detail how they fit into the existing space. Here, two shallow drawers in the preparation table hold utensils, while a trash can sits between its legs. Deep pot and pan drawers and a slim drawer for cooking oils flank the oven.

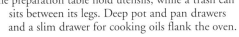

❹ BOOKSHELF AND TABLE ▷
The door opens onto the right-hand wall so this area is kept simple to avoid obstructing the entrance. Select a sturdy, wall-mounted bookshelf, bulletin board, kitchen table, and wall covering, on the basis that this area of the room may be susceptible to bumps.

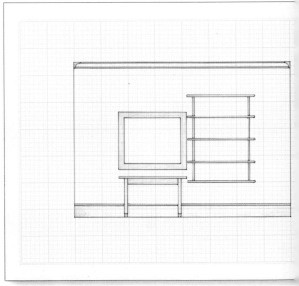

◁ STORE SAMPLES
Collect paint color, tile, and countertop samples from DIY and interior design shops to help you build up a picture of your finished kitchen.

REFER TO CATALOGS ▷
Keep the catalogs that feature your
chosen appliances and materials
handy, to help you budget and as
a source of local distributors and
suppliers for placing your orders.

◁ ❷ SINK ELEVATION
Focus on the sink cabinet and pay
attention to detail, such as the choice
of materials for the sink basin, cabinet
doors, faucets, drainboards, dishwasher
casing, and the wall cabinet. Also think
about the flooring for this wet area, a
backsplash behind the sink to protect
the walls, lighting, and curtains.

WHAT NEXT?

■ Take your finished
design to a major kitchen
manufacturer, a specialized
kitchen design company, or
a local cabinetmaker. They
can check your plans and
provide technical information.

■ Obtain construction permits
from relevant authorities for
any structural changes.

■ Coordination of the work
is important. Agree a schedule
with the builders, plumbers,
electricians, installers, and the
decorators involved. The
order of work is as follows:
structural alterations; wiring
and plumbing; floor-laying;
basecoat decoration; cabinet-
installation, and then the
final electrical, plumbing, and
decoration work.

■ Check that the delivery
dates for appliances,
cabinets, and materials
meet your work schedule.

■ When you know how
long the job will take, set up a
temporary kitchen or make
other eating arrangements.

△ **LIGHT FIXTURES**
Work out a lighting
plan and fix the wiring
before the kitchen is
installed. Attach light
fixtures when the room
is almost finished.

▽ **FLOOR PLAN**
A bird's-eye view shows you exactly
how the kitchen elements are placed
in relation to the shape of the room.

△ ❸ **FIXED FEATURES**
Plot fixed features, such as the built-in
cabinet and window, to check how much
space is available for a table and chairs in
front of these features. Draw
the dishwasher stack in profile to be
sure the cabinet doors can
open fully without any
obstruction.

BUDGET TIPS

■ After producing your initial
design, work out how much
appliances, cabinets, flooring
and other materials will cost.
Obtain estimates for building,
plumbing, and electrical work
that need to be done to help
you calculate the costs of
installing your new kitchen.

■ If your ideal kitchen design
is beyond your budget, see
where you can cut expenses.
Perhaps you can reduce the
scale of building work, select
less expensive flooring and
countertops, and use fewer
good quality cabinets.

■ Allow some room in the
budget to cover unexpected
costs that may arise.

FABRICS AND FINISHES ▷
When planning your budget, allow
money for finishing decoration and
furnishings. Quality curtain fabrics
and wood cabinet finishes add extra
comfort and warmth to the kitchen.

USEFUL ADDRESSES

The following directory of useful names and addresses will help you source the products needed to furnish and equip your kitchen.

PROFESSIONAL ASSOCIATIONS

AMERICAN GAS ASSOCIATION
1515 Wilson Blvd.
Arlington, VA 22209
Tel: (703) 841-8400
Fax: (703) 841-8406
National association for information on gas appliances in the home.

AMERICAN LIGHTING ASSOCIATION
P. O. Box 420288
World Trade Center, Suite 10046
Dallas, TX 45342-0288
Tel: (214) 698-9898
Tel: (800) 605-4448
Fax: (214) 698-9899
National association of lighting manufacturers.

AMERICAN SOCIETY OF INTERIOR DESIGNERS
608 Massachusetts Ave. NE
Washington, DC 20002-6006
Tel: (202) 546-3480
Fax: (202) 546-3240
National association of interior designers.

ASSOCIATION OF HOME APPLIANCE MANUFACTURERS
20 N. Wacker Drive
Chicago, IL 60606
Tel: (312) 984-5800
Fax: (312) 984-5823
National association of home appliance manufacturers.

NATIONAL KITCHEN AND BATH ASSOCIATION
687 Willow Grove Street
Hackettstown, NJ 07840
Tel: (800) 843-6522
National association of kitchen and bathroom designers, and manufacturers of kitchen and bathroom products.

KITCHEN FURNITURE AND EQUIPMENT

ADELPHI CUSTOM CABINETRY
P. O. Box 10
Robesonia, PA 19551
Tel: (800) 992-3101
Custom cabinetry for kitchens, living rooms, family rooms, bedrooms, etc.

ALSTO'S HANDY HELPERS
P. O. Box 1267
Galesburg, IL 61402
Tel: (800) 447-0048
Fax: (800) 522 5786
Kitchen furniture and accessories; phone for a catalog.

COLONIAL GARDEN KITCHENS
Dept CGZ4183
Hanover, PA 17333-0066
Tel: (800) 323-6000
Kitchen equipment, appliances, and gadgetry for the home; phone and mail orders.

CRATE & BARREL
Tel: (888) 249-4158
Home furnishings and equipment; call for catalog and addresses of retail stores.

EUROPEAN COUNTRY KITCHEN
49 Route 202 P. O. Box 117
Far Hills, NJ 07931
Tel: (908) 781-1554
Fax: (908) 781-1543
Traditional cabinetry for kitchens, bedrooms, and bathrooms.

JOHNNY GREY & CO. USA
49 Route 202
Far Hills, NJ 07931
Tel: (800) 517-3651
Individually designed kitchens and freestanding furniture.

JOHNNY GREY & CO. USA
c/o Cambium
119 West Hubbard Street
Chicago, IL 60610
Tel: (312) 832 9920
Fax: (312) 832 9923
Individually designed kitchens and freestanding furniture.

HOME DEPOT
Corporate Offices
2727 Paces Ferry Road
Atlanta, GA 30339
Tel: (800) 553-3199
Nationwide chain of home supply stores; call for catalog, product information, and addresses of retail outlets.

KAPLAN BROTHERS BLUE FLAME CORP.
523 West 125th Street
New York, NY 10027-3498
Tel: (800) 528-6913
Tel: (212) 662-6990
Fax: (212) 663-2026
Chef-quality commercial kitchen equipment, including Garland stoves, Dynamic cooking systems, Vulcan products; phone and mail orders.

KRAFTMAID CABINETRY
Middlefield, OH 44062
Tel: (216) 632-5333
http://www.kraftmaid.com
Custom cabinetry for the home.

MERILLAT INDUSTRIES, INC.
MASCO Corp.
P. O. Box 1946
5353 West US 223
Adrian, MI 49921
Tel: (517) 263-0771
Fax: (517) 263-4792
Custom cabinetry for kitchens, living rooms/family rooms, etc.

PIER 1 IMPORTS
Tel: (800) 447-4371
Small items for kitchens; call for retail store locations.

PINE FACTORY
P. O. Drawer 672
Ashland, VA 23005
Tel: (804) 796-9156
Pine kitchen furniture; phone and mail orders.

POTTERY BARN
Mail Order Department
P. O. Box 7044
San Francisco, CA 94120-7044
Tel: (800) 922-5507
Kitchen furniture and accessories; phone and mail orders; call for catalog and details of stores.

RENOVATOR'S SUPPLY
P. O. Box 2515
Conway, NH 03818-2515
Tel: (800) 922-5507
Tel: (800) 659-2211
Specialists in reproduction sinks, fittings, lighting etc., for kitchens and bathrooms.

SNAIDERO INTERNATIONAL USA, INC.

201 West 132nd Street
Los Angeles, CA 90061
Tel: (310) 516-8499
Fax: (310) 516-9918
http://www.snaidero.it
Custom cabinetry for the home.

WICKER WAREHOUSE, INC.

195 South River Street
Hackensack, NJ 07601
Tel: (800) 989-4253
Tel: (201) 342-6709
Fax: (201) 342-1495
Wicker furniture; phone and mail orders.

YIELD HOUSE

P. O. Box 2525
Conway, NH 03818-2515
Tel: (800) 659-0206

Largest furniture mail order house in US; kits available for home builders; phone for catalog.

MAJOR APPLIANCE MANUFACTURERS

AMANA HOME APPLIANCES

2800 220th Trail
P. O. Box 8901
Amana, IA 52204-0001
Tel: (800) 843-0304
Ranges, cooktops, refrigerator/freezers, dishwashers, microwaves, and air conditioners.

COLE'S APPLIANCE & FURNITURE CO.

4026 Lincoln Ave.
Chicago, Il 60618-3097
Tel: (773) 525-1797
Major appliances, electronics, home furnishing, and bedding. Price quotes available.

DIAL-A-BRAND, INC.

57 South Main Street
Freeport, NY 11520
Tel: (516) 378-9694
Fax: (516) 867-3447
Major home appliances and electronics. Manufacturer's name and model number required for price quotes; phone and mail orders.

EBA WHOLESALE

2361 Nostrand Ave.
Brooklyn, NY 11210
Tel: (800) 380-2378
Tel: (718) 252-3400
Fax: (718) 253-6002
Major kitchen appliances; call for current special offerings; phone and mail orders.

FRIGIDAIRE CO.

P. O. Box 7181
Dublin, OH 43017
Tel: (800) 685-6005
Ranges, cooktops, refrigerator/freezers, dishwashers, microwaves, air conditioners. Presently offers the only front-loading clothes washer and matching dryer available in the U.S.

GAGGENAU USA CORP.

425 University Ave.
Norwood, MA 02062
Tel: (617) 255-1766
Cooktops, steamers, and ovens made in Germany.

GE APPLIANCES

General Electric
AP 35 - Room 1007B
Appliance Park
Louisville, KY 40225
Tel: (800) 626-2000
Tel: (502) 452-4557
Ranges, cooktops, refrigerator/freezers, dishwashers, microwaves, and air conditioners.

GRINGER & SONS

29 First Avenue
New York, NY 10003
Tel: (212) 475-0600
Fax: (212) 982-1935
Major household appliances; phone and mail orders.

JENN-AIR

240 Edwards Street SE
Cleveland, TN 37311
(800) JENN-AIR
Tel: (800) 536-6247
http://www.jennair.com
Maker of all major household appliances. Unique "down-draft system" on ranges and cooktops allows indoor grilling with venting of fumes to outdoors.

KITCHENAID

2000 M-63
Mail Drop 4302
Benton Harbor, MI 49022
Tel: (800) 253-3977
Tel: (616) 923-5000
Fax: (616) 923-3214
Ranges, cooktops, refrigerator/freezers, dishwashers, microwaves, air conditioners; trash compactors, and food garbage disposal units also available.

LVT PRICE QUOTE HOTLINE, INC.

Box 444-W97
Commack, NY 11725-0444
Tel: (516) 234-8884
Fax: (516) 234-8808
E-mail: callvt@aol.com
Over 4,000 household appliances and home electronics. Shipping charges included in price quote; phone, fax, and mail orders.

MAYTAG CO.

403 West 4th Street North
Newton, IA 50208
Tel: (800) 688-9900
Ranges, cooktops, refrigerator/freezers, dishwashers, microwaves, and air conditioners, including Magic Chef and Admiral brands.

MIELE APPLIANCES

22D World's Fair Drive
Somerset NH 08873
Tel: (800) 843-7231
Ranges, cooktops, refrigerator/freezers, dishwashers, microwaves, and air conditioners.

PERCY'S, INC.

Gold Star Blvd.
Worcester, MA 01605
Tel: (800) 922-8194
Fax: (508) 797-5578
E-mail: alanl@percys.com
Major appliances; phone and mail orders.

SUB-ZERO FREEZER CO. INC.

P. O. Box 44130
Madison, WI 53744-4130
Tel: (800) 444-7820
Tel: (608) 271-2233
Fax: (608) 271-7471
Combination refrigerator/freezers in a wide array of finishes, door styles, and dimensions.

TAPPAN APPLIANCES

6000 Perimeter Drive
Dublin, OH 43017
Tel: (800) 685-6005
Fax: (614) 792-4073
Ranges, cooktops, refrigerator/freezers, dishwashers, microwaves, and air conditioners.

THERMADOR, MASCO CORP.

5119 District Blvd.
Los Angeles, CA 90040
Tel: (213) 562-1133
Fax: (213) 560-1788
Ranges, cooktops, refrigerator/freezers, dishwashers, microwaves, and air conditioners.

VIKING RANGE CORP.
111 Front Street
Greenwood, MS 38930
Tel: (601) 455-1200
Fax: (601) 453-7939
Speciality, professional-quality cooking ranges.

WHIRLPOOL CORP.
2000 M-63
Mail Drop 4303
Benton Harbor, MI 49022
Tel: (800) 253-1301
Ranges, cooktops, refrigerator/freezers, dishwashers, microwaves, and air conditioners.

WHITE-WESTINGHOUSE, FRIGIDAIRE CO.
6000 Perimeter Drive
Dublin, OH 43017
Tel: (800) 374-4434
Tel: (614) 792-4102
Fax: (614) 792-4079
http://www.frigidaire.com
Ranges, cooktops, refrigerator/freezers, dishwashers, microwaves, and air conditioners.

SINKS & FAUCETS
American Standard, Inc.
P. O. Box 6820
One Centennial Plaza
Piscataway, NJ 08855
Tel: (800) 752-6292
Tel: (908) 980-3000
Call for catalog, product information, and referrals to retail sources.

DELTA FAUCET
Masco Corporation
55 East 111 Street
Indianapolis, IN 46280
Tel: (317) 848-1812
Fax: (317) 573-3486
Call or fax for catalog, product information, and referrals to retail sources.

EGO AMENITIES
74 Montauk Highway
Red Horse Plaza
East Hampton, NY 11937
Tel: (526) 329-9149
Fax: (516) 329-5233
Speciality showroom for kitchen sinks and faucets.

ELJER PLUMBINGWARE
17120 Dallas Parkway
Dallas, TX 75248
Tel: (972) 407-2600
Fax: (972) 407-2789
Call or fax for catalog, product information, and referrals to retail sources.

EUROPEAN COUNTRY COOKING
P. O. Box 154
Oldwick, NJ 08858
Tel: (800) 883-5339
Tel: (908) 236-7337
Custom and special-order sinks and faucets.

FRANKE, INC. KITCHEN SYSTEMS
212 Church Road
North Wales, PA 19454
Tel: (800) 626-5771
Tel: (215) 699-8761
Fax: (215) 661-8258
Call or fax for catalog, product information, and referrals to retail sources.

KOHLER CO.
444 Highland Drive
Kohler, WI 53044
Tel: (800) 456-4537
Tel: (414) 457-4441
Phone for catalog, and referrals to retail sources.

MOEN, INC.
Master Brand Industries, Inc.
25300 Al Moen Drive
North Olmstead, OH 44070-8022
Tel: (800) 553-6636
Tel: (216) 962-200
Fax: (216) 962-2772
Call or fax for catalog, product information, and referrals to retail sources.

COUNTERTOPS AND WORK SURFACES

DUPONT CORIAN
Chestnut Run Plaza
P. O. Box 80702
Wilmington, DE 19880-0702
Tel: (800) 426-7426
Fax: (302) 999-2356
Sculptable synthetic countertops.

FORMICA CORPORATION
10155 Reading Road
Cincinnati, OH 45241-5729
Tel: (800) 367-6422
Tel: (513) 786-3533
Fax: (513) 786-3024
Laminate surfacing for countertops and cabinets, and other products.

WILSONART INTERNATIONAL
2400 Wilson Place
Temple, TX 76504
Tel: (800) 433-3222
Tel: (817) 778-2711
Fax: (817) 770-2384
Laminate surfacing for countertops and cabinets.

STONE SURFACES
80 Willow Street
East Rutherford, NJ 07073
Tel: (201) 935-8803
Fax: (201) 935-8210
Stone counters, island tops, tabletops, etc.

TRANSOLID, INC.
Solid Surface Solutions
11515 Vanstory Drive
Huntersville, NC 28078
Tel: (704) 948-1927
Fax: (704) 948-9027
Solid-material countertops and other products.

WINDOW AND WALL COVERINGS

AMERICAN BLIND & WALLPAPER FACTORY
909 North Sheldon Road
Plymouth, MI 48170
Tel: (800) 735-5300
Design consultations; phone and mail orders.

AMERICAN DISCOUNT WALL & WINDOW COVERINGS
1411 Fifth Ave.
Pittsburgh, PA 15219
Tel: (800) 777-2737
Fax: (412) 232-4683
Custom upholstery and decorator fabrics; phone, fax, and mail orders.

FABRACADABRICS
27 Leigh Street
Clinton, NJ 08809
Tel: (908) 735-4757
Fax: (908) 730-9707
Custom upholstery made-to-order.

HANCOCK'S
3841 Hinkleville Road
Paducah, KY 42001
Tel: (800) 845-8723
Fax: (502) 442-2164
E-mail: DsingBear@aol.com
Catalog offers best-selling designer/decorator fabrics at substantial savings; phone, fax, and mail orders.

NATIONAL BLIND & WALLPAPER FACTORY
400 Galleria # 400
Southfield, MI 48034
Tel: (800) 477-8000
Window treatments and wall coverings; phone and mail orders.

Floor Coverings

American Olean Tile Co.
1000 Cannon Ave.
Lansdale, PA 19446
Tel: (215) 855-1111
Domestically manufactured ceramic tiles.

Armstrong World Industries, Inc.
Adistra Corp.
101 Union Street
Plymouth, MI 48170
Tel: (800) 704-8000
Vinyl flooring and other products.

Congoleum
Princeton Pike Corporate Center #1
989 Lenox Drive
Lawrenceville, NJ 08648
Tel: (800) 934-3567
Vinyl flooring and other products.

Country Floors
15 East 16th Street
New York, NY 10003
Tel: (212) 627-8300
Fax: (212) 627-7442
http://www. countryfloors.com
Imported ceramic tile; hand-painted and custom tile designs.

Kahrs Swedish Prefinished Wood Floors
Tel: (800) 784-8523
Call for product information and local stores.

Mannington Wood Floors
Mannington Mills, Inc.
1327 Lincoln Drive
High Pond, NC 27260
Tel: (800) 252-4202
Tel: (919) 884-5600
Fax (919) 812-4975
Wooden flooring; parquetry supplies, also vinyl flooring, and other products.

Ann Sacks Tile and Stone
8120 NE 33rd Drive
Portland, OR 97211
Tel: (503) 281-7751
Fax: (503) 287-8807
Special-order and custom tiles; stone and surface design service.

Tarkett
800 Lanidex Plaza
Parsippany, NJ 07054
Tel: (800) 827-5388
Fax: (201) 428-8017
Vinyl flooring and other products.

Lighting

Elkay Manufacturing Company
2222 Camden Court
Oak Brook, IL 60521
Tel: (630) 574-8484
Specialized and also general kitchen lighting.

Golden Valley Lighting
274 Eastchester Drive
High Point, NC 27262
Tel: (800) 735-3377
Specialized and general kitchen lighting.

Task Lighting Corporation
P. O. Box 1090
910 East 25th Street
Kearney, NE 68848-1090
Tel: (800) 445-6404
Tel: (308) 236-6707
Fax: (308) 234-9401
Design and manufacture of lighting systems for the kitchen.

Hardware

Jaeggers
22 Third Avenue
Long Branch, NJ 07740
Tel: (908) 870-8980
Fax: (908) 870-2516
Specialists in knobs, handles, register covers, etc.

Smith Woodworks and Design
101 Farmersville Road
Califon, NJ 07830
Tel: (908) 832-2723
Fax: (908) 832-6994
Wooden knobs, handles, covers for switchplates and outlets.

Kraft
306 East 61st Street
New York, NY 10021
Tel: (212) 838-2214
Fax: (212) 644-9254
Full-service hardware supplier; fax and phone orders; price quotes and special orders.

Standard of Lynn
400 Lynn Way
P. O. Box 830
Lynn, MA 01903
Tel: (800) 590-5090
Fax: (800) 590-5091
Hardware design and manufacturing.

Speciality Products

CalorQue Ltd.
2380 Cranberry Highway
West Wareham, MA 02576
Tel: (508) 291-4224
Fax: (508) 291-2299
E-mail: heat@caloriq.ultranet.com
In-floor heating systems.

Dome-It Dome Ceilings
2025 J&C Blvd #6
Naples, Fl 33942-6213
Tel: (800) 771-3663
Tel: (813) 591-0607
Fax: (813) 566-3932
Dome ceilings and skylights.

Domotek
176 Abbeywood Circle, Suite 100
Streamwood, IL 60107
Tel: (708) 736-3136
Fax: (708) 736-7443
In-floor heating systems.

J & M Air, Inc.
189 South Bridge Street
Somerville, NJ 08876
Tel: (908) 707-4040
Fax: (908) 707-0447
Custom stainless-steel installations, counters, walls, and partitions.

David H. Little, Artist-Blacksmith
Winnepesaukee Forge, Inc.
31 Foundry Ave., Unit 6
Merideth, NH 03253
Tel: (603) 279-5492
Fax: (603) 279-4293
Hand-crafted wrought ironwork.

J. M. Originals
P. O. Box 482
Gladstone, NJ 07934
Tel: (908) 879-6728
Specialized custom interior painting projects.

Pittsburgh Corning Glass Block Products
P. O. Box 3900
Peoria, IL 61612
Tel: (800) 624-2120
Manufacturers and suppliers of architectural glass blocks.

INDEX

ACKNOWLEDGMENTS

AUTHOR'S ACKNOWLEDGMENTS

I would like to thank all those who allowed us into their homes to photograph their kitchens, particularly my clients Nick and Joan Marmont, Nick and Susie Ussiskin, and my wife Becca, and in addition, Mr and Mrs Miles, Julia and Nick Parker, and also Mark and Sara Quinn-Wilson.

Special gratitude is due to the craftsmen with whom I've worked over the years, their skill, spirit, and hard work turning my kitchen ideas into beautifully made furniture. They include, amongst many others, Jonathan Morriss, Stephen Cordell, Gordon Hopkins, Jonathan Parlett, Miles Muggleton, Andrew Parslow, Nigel Brown, Patrick Warnes, Paul Jobst, Paul Saban, John Barnard and Robin Weeks, specialist painters Jenny Holt, Felix Delmar, and the artist Lucy Turner.

My own design team too, deserve much credit for their hard work and enthusiasm – David Richards, Lynne Fornieles, Mike Rooke, Will Jameson, Anna Moore, and Richard Lee who also conceived the beautifully detailed kitchen illustrations that feature throughout the book.

I owe a special thanks to the team at Dorling Kindersley. First of all to Mary-Clare Jerram and Amanda Lunn who persuaded me to write the book, to Colin Walton who designed it so carefully and provided art direction, and to my brave editor Bella Pringle, who deserves a great deal of credit for her hard work and skill. Many thanks also to photographer Peter Anderson for his careful eye, his patience, and his hard work.

Finally, heartfelt thanks to my wife who put up with my absence at crucial periods of family life, to allow me the time to write two books at once, and still provide encouragement when needed.

PUBLISHER'S ACKNOWLEDGMENTS

Dorling Kindersley would also like to thank: Rebecca and Johnny Grey, Nick and Joan Marmont, Mr and Mrs Miles, Julia and Nick Parker, Nick and Susie Ussiskin, and Mark and Sara Quinn-Wilson for allowing us to photograph their kitchens.

Thank you also to the following kitchen showrooms who granted us permission to photograph on their premises: Arc Linea; Bulthaup; Chalon; C.P. Hart; Newcastle Furniture Company; Nicholas Anthony, and to Fired Earth, for use of their floorings.

We are also grateful to those who kindly supplied props: American Appliance Centre; Amtico; Christoph Caffyn; La Cuisinière; David Mellor; Formica Ltd; Geneviève Lethu; Graham & Green; Hogarth & Dwyer; Jerry's Home Store; Mediterranean Imports; Moore Park Delicatessen; Pallam Precast; P.G. Kitchens & Bathrooms; RJ's HomeShop; Sinclair Till, and Viaduct Furniture Ltd.

Special thanks also goes to: Jeremy Myerson for helping us to establish this series, Phillip Hayes, UK managing director of Siematic kitchens, for his time and helpful advice; to Charlotte Davies and Clive Hayball for their guidance throughout the project; to Angeles Gavira and Simon Maughan for editorial assistance; to Ann Kay for proof-reading; and to Hilary Bird for the index.

ARTWORK: Richard Lee

PHOTOGRAPHY:

All photographs by Peter Anderson and Matthew Ward except:
(Kitchen designers are named in brackets.)
Peter Aprahamian (Johnny Grey) 10, 52–53; Interior Archive / Tim Beddow (John Pawson) 56bl; Simon Brown (Johnny Grey) 57; Michael Focard (Johnny Grey) 65; Ray Main 8bl, 52tl, and 52bl, 60tl, 61, 64tr; Diana Miller 8t, 37tr, 85t; James Mortimer (Johnny Grey) 6b; David Parmiter (Claudia Bryant) 52br, 56tr and 56br; Colin Radcliffe Design 64bl; Trevor Richards (Johnny Grey) 6, 9, 40cl, 64tl and 64br, 72br; Paul Ryan / International Interiors (Fell-Clark Design) 68bl; Paul Ryan / International Interiors (Gerry Nelisson) 68br; Deidi von Schaewen 68tl; Fritz von der Schulenberg (Nico Rensch) 46cl; Colin Walton 40bl, 43tr, 76br, 77tr, 78–79b, 80tl, 87b.

The following companies kindly lent us their photographs: Aga-Rayburn 13tl, 30t; Alternative Plans 37b; Chalon 56bl; Jenn-Air (CV4380PG) 28t, (WW27210PG) 31bl, (SVD8310PG) 82; John Lewis of Hungerford 72tr; Kohler 27b; Newcastle Furniture Company 56tl; Snaidero 52cb; Sub-zero 20bl; Wrighton Kitchens 'Albany' (Texas Homecare and selected Homebase stores) 44l.

Every effort has been made to trace the copyright holders. We apologise for any unintentional omission and would be pleased to insert these in subsequent editions.

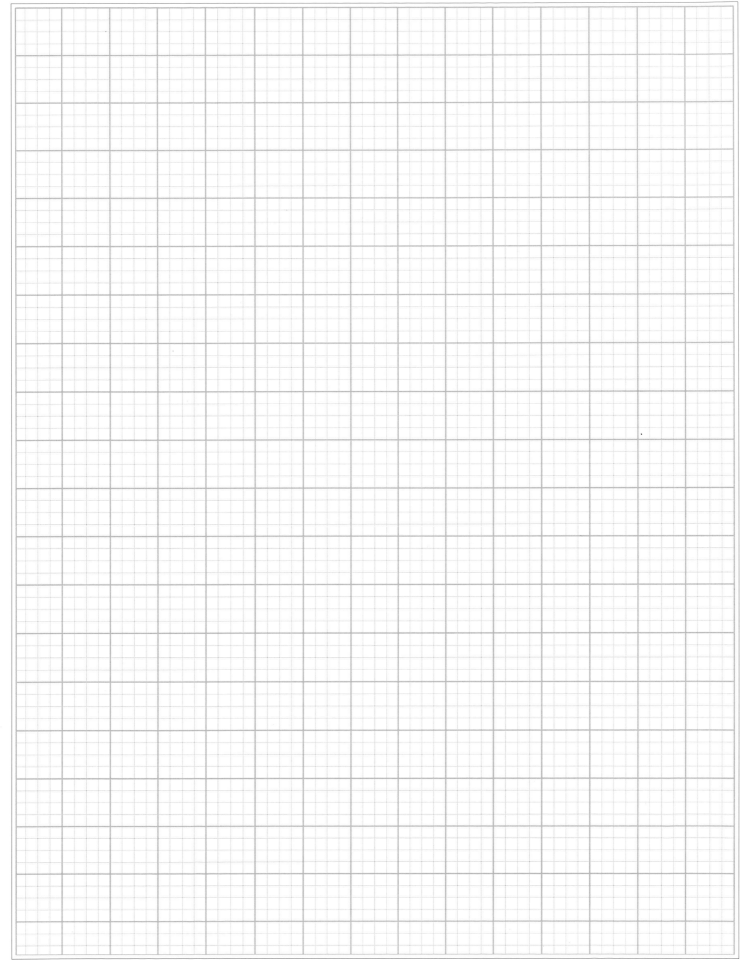

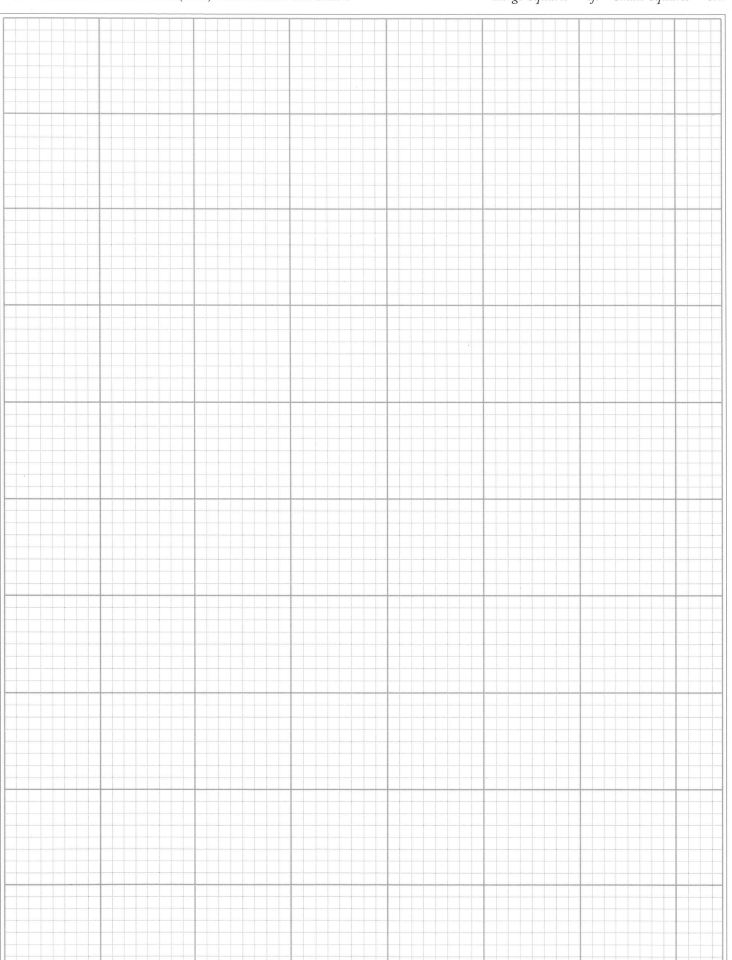

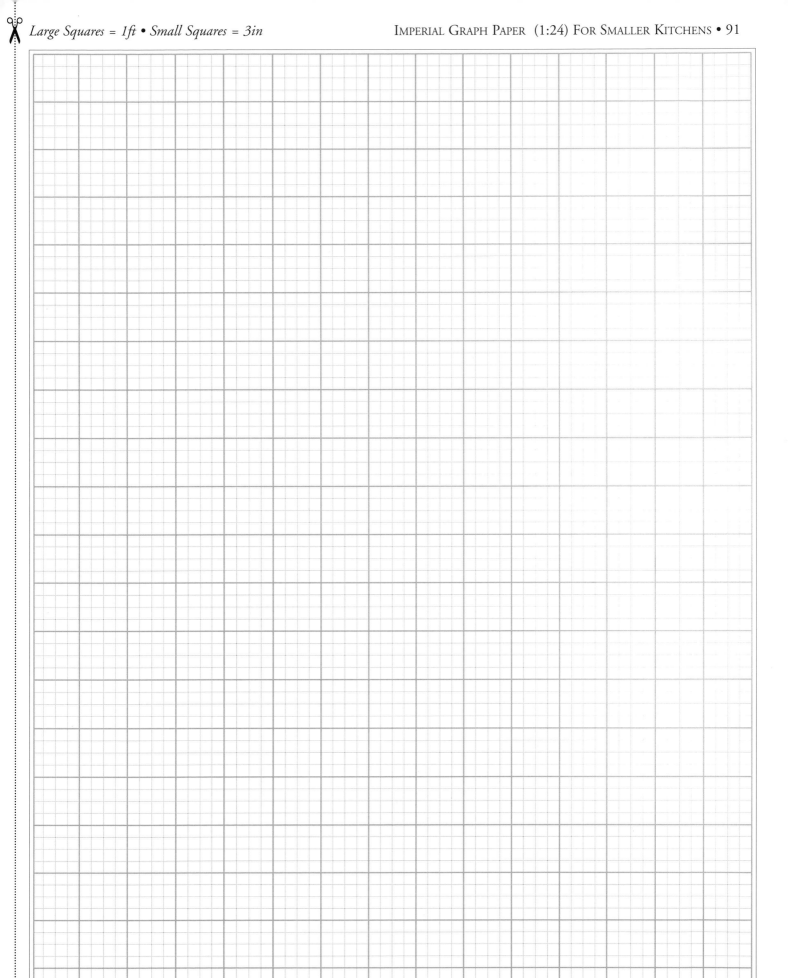

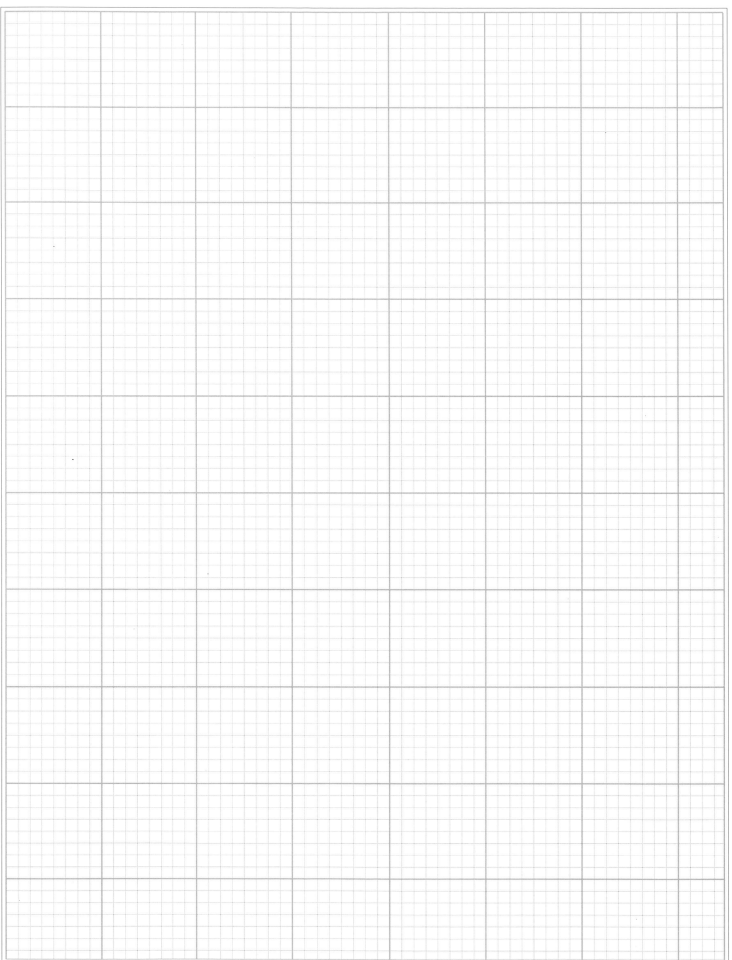

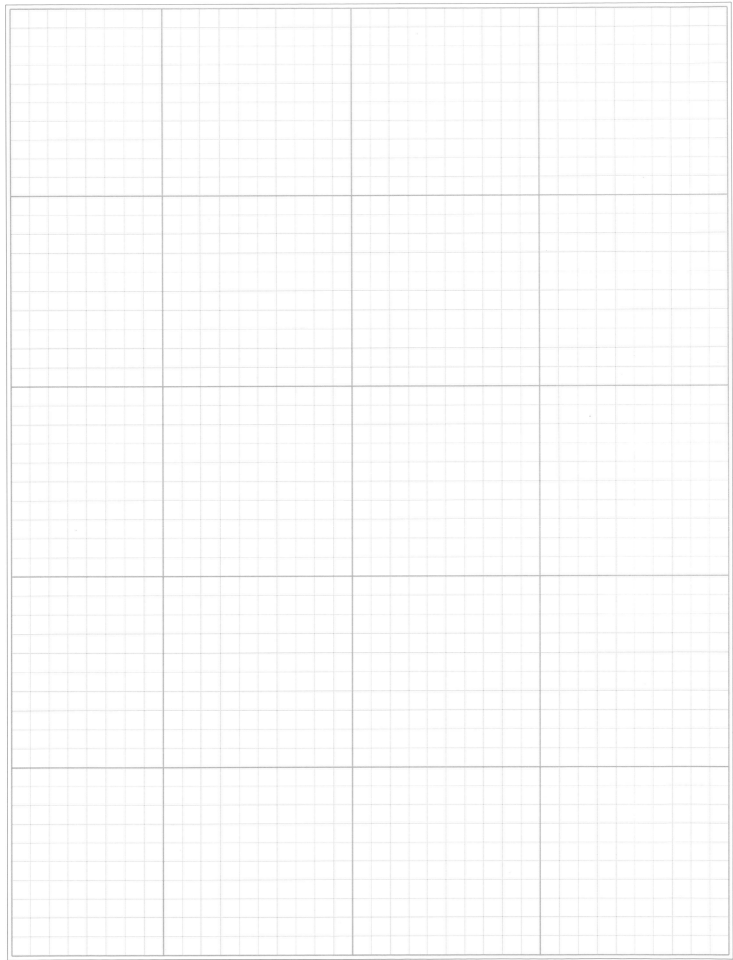

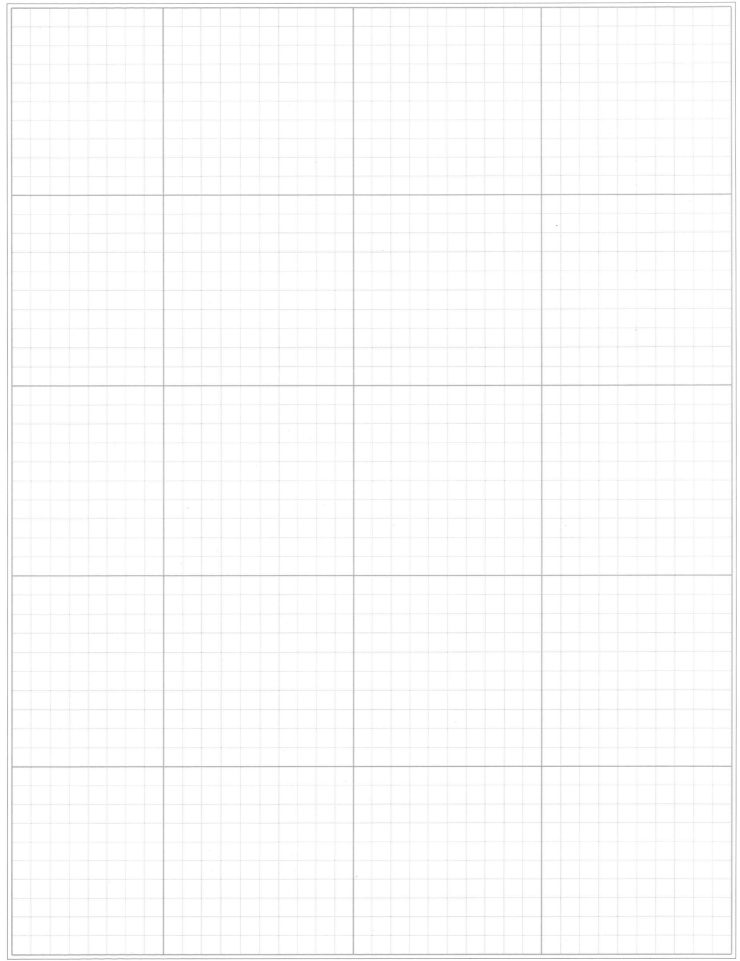